SLAVERY

DISCUSSED IN

OCCASIONAL ESSAYS,

FROM 1833 TO 1846.

SLAVERY

DISCUSSED IN

OCCASIONAL ESSAYS,

FROM 1833 TO 1846.

BY

LEONARD BACON,

PASTOR OF THE FIRST CHURCH IN NEW HAVEN.

MNEMOSYNE PUBLISHING CO., INC.
MIAMI, FLORIDA
1969

Originally Published in New York 1846

First Mnemosyne reprinting 1969

Reprinted from a copy in the
Fisk University Library Negro Collection.

Copyright © 1969   Mnemosyne Publishing Co., Inc.   Miami, Florida

Library of Congress Catalog Card Number:

70-83954

Printed in the United States of America

PREFACE.

SEVERAL years before the commencement of the Anti-Slavery agitation on this side of the Atlantic, it so happened that I was led to consider, with some care, the condition and prospects of the enslaved class in the United States. From that time to the present, no subject not immediately connected with my official duties or my professional studies, has occupied so much of my attention. When the British Anti-Slavery Societies began their labors, in 1823, I entered into their views as then exhibited; and I learned much from the reports of those Societies, and from the pamphlets published by Stephens, Clarkson, Wilberforce and others. When the Rev. Joshua Leavitt, now so eminent among American abolitionists, made his first appearance as a writer on slavery, in 1825, I agreed generally with his views, and was instructed by his arguments; for his views, at that time, were substantially the same with those which the British abolitionists were then urging upon Parliament. From him I learned

to make certain distinctions which still seem to me
essential to any just view of the subject, widely as
he and others have since departed from them.*

---

* After the lapse of one and twenty years, it cannot seem indelicate
to refer to Mr. Leavitt as the author of the articles above alluded to.
They were published in the Christian Spectator for 1825, pp. 130-138,
239-246. I well remember the violent sensation which they produced
in Charleston, where the Christian Spectator was immediately put upon
the *Index librorum prohibitorum* of his holiness Judge Lynch. Yet
those articles were far from containing the modern Anti-Slavery doctrine. Witness such passages as these :

" The right of personal liberty is not, in all circumstances, an *absolute* right. If it were so, slavery would have never been recognized
in the Word of God. Yet it was permitted and regulated in the laws
given by God himself Lev. xxv. 44, 45." "Neither has Christianity
interfered in this respect to abolish slavery. Paul has given directions
for the mutual deportment of masters and servants, or slaves, as they
were in those days."—p. 131.

" Our own laws recognize involuntary servitude whenever the public
good and the interest of the individual require it. Such is substantially
the case of minors, of idiots, of spendthrifts, of drunkards. The right
of personal liberty, therefore, is not one which may be lawfully vindi-
cated *at all hazards*. *Salus populi, suprema lex. The public good*, the
interest of all classes, both whites and blacks, is *the supreme law*.
Slaves have no more an abstract absolute right to rise and kill their
masters, and involve the *whole* community in destruction, than the son
or apprentice has to revolt from the control under which the laws have
placed him. The very idea is most preposterous, that a part of the
community have a right, which they may assert to the destruction of
the peace and happiness of the whole. The right of the master, therefore, to the services of his slave, *may be* as perfect as to the services
of his apprentice. But this right depends, in either case, wholly on
the assumed fact, that in existing circumstances the public good requires the existence of servitude. It is a mere creature of society,
and depends entirely upon the laws."—pp. 131-132.

In the year 1830, or soon after, a new doctrine, or what seemed such, began to be current. The English Anti-Slavery Societies, in the heat of their con-

---

"I have had three objects in view, in thus going into the nature of slavery as a legal institution. In the first place, I wish it to appear that the relation between the master and slaves, is a proper subject of legislation. It is a conventional right and depends entirely upon the laws."—*ibid.*

"The second object was to relieve slaveholders from a charge, or an apprehension of criminality, where in fact there is no offence. There can be no palliation for the conduct of those who first brought the curse of slavery upon poor Africa, and America too. But the body of the present generation are not liable to this charge. Posterity are not answerable for the sins of their fathers, unless they approve their deeds. They found the negroes among them, in a degraded state, incapable either of appreciating or enjoying liberty. They have, therefore, nothing to answer for on this score, because they have no other alternative, *at present*, but to keep them in subjection. There is nothing so destructive to the moral sense, as to be forced, by our principles, to the acknowledgment of guilt, in that which we at the same time believe to be absolutely unavoidable, and in which, therefore, it is impossible really to feel self-reproach." "A Christian *may* hold slaves, and exact their services, without any occasion to feel a pang of self-reproach *merely on account* of his holding slaves."—p. 133.

"The third object aimed at, was to fasten the charge of criminality on the very spot where such a charge will lie, and where it ought to be felt; and where alone reformation is practicable. There are no duties without corresponding rights, and no rights without corresponding duties. While it is the duty of the slave to submit himself to his own master so long as the laws of this country make him a slave, it is his right to be protected *by the laws*, in the enjoyment of life, health, chastity, good name, and every blessing which he can enjoy consistently with the public welfare."

"Christianity enforces this dictate of sound reason. 'Thou shalt love thy neighbor as thyself,' is as much the law between master and

1*

flict with the " West India interest," being most rea-
sonably disgusted with the resistance of the colonial
authorities to every measure that had any tendency
towards freedom, had begun to renounce all further
dependence upon such measures, and to demand of
Parliament the immediate abolition of slavery. "*Immediate abolition*" had become the popular doctrine
among philanthropists; and "gradualism" or the
notion of a process of abolition, was scouted as an
obsolete idea. Accordingly the doctrine of immediate abolition began to be current here; but here it
was necessarily, to some extent at least, another thing
from what it was in Great Britain. There it was a
demand that a new constitution of society, a new
body of laws, a new system of relations between
capital and labor, and between the landholder and
the peasant, should be imposed upon dependent and
vassal colonies by the omnipotence of the Imperial
Parliament. Here it became the doctrine of "imme-

---

slave, as between any other members of the human family. This is so
obvious as to appear almost like a truism. And yet this is the very
thing that has always been lost sight of among slaveholders. It has
been wholly disregarded in our own nation." "We do not answer
to this indictment unless we either plead guilty, or show that our *laws*,
our customs, our modes of thinking and acting, recognize the humanity of the negroes."—pp. 133, 134.

Some of these statements are no doubt unguarded. But the leading
principles and distinctions carried conviction to my mind at the time;
and it still seems to me that there can be no just reasoning on the subject without them.

diate *emancipation*" by individual masters, " at all hazards," and without regard to consequences; the doctrine that slavery is a sin on the part of the master, always and in all circumstances, and that he must immediately renounce his authority without asking what is expedient for the commonwealth, or what for the welfare of the slave. All who refused to receive that doctrine and its corollaries, were denounced as " pro-slavery," and as sacrificing duty to expediency.

Such was the occasion on which I felt myself called to publish the first of the following essays. A critical examination of the subject in the light of the Scriptures, seemed to be necessary at that time; and I did what I could. The two or three years that followed, were years of great excitement in respect to slavery. The most extravagant views were presented on both sides. On the one hand, the Anti-Slavery party, including the no-government element from which it has now in some measure disengaged itself, seemed to aim at irritating public opinion into phrenzy. On the other hand, the southern people were demanding that the discussion of slavery in the free States should be put down by mobs; and there were found northern men base enough to lend themselves to such a demand. The dates of several of these essays, will show that they were written during that period of excitement.

Ten years ago, I thought that I had done all that it was my duty to do in this way. But within a few months past, a sort of necessity seems to be laid upon me. The subject came up, last summer, in the General Association of the Congregational Pastors of Connecticut. And there, as I have always been wont to do wherever an opportunity has arisen, I expressed very freely the same views which I had formerly uttered through the press. What I said, in the freedom of fraternal debate, was reported, not very accurately, in several newspapers; and some of those reports were commented upon with severity in the " Christian Observer," a Presbyterian newspaper, which, though published in Philadelphia, seems to be designed chiefly for a southern circulation. Thus summoned before the public, I could not well refuse to answer for myself. Then came the proceedings in the American Board of Foreign Missions; and the extent to which I found myself involved in that debate, and in the newspaper discussions which followed, seemed to require that I should not excuse myself from one more attempt to vindicate what is manifest to my mind as truth.

Nothing is more likely, than that some differences may be discovered between the earlier essays and the later, for the Author has intended to regard truth rather than his own consistency, and he will not undertake to maintain that, in thirteen years he has learned nothing. The only changes made, besides the removal of some verbal inaccuracies, incident to the haste of writing for a periodical publication, are the correction of one passage which when first published, gave unintentional offence, and the omission of two or three allusions, in the earlier essays, to the controversy which the Anti-Slavery Society was then maintaining with the friends of African colonization. That controversy, since our Anti-Slavery friends have done so much at colonization in Canada, seems to be at rest; and I have no wish to revive it.

Some of my friends have expected that I would reply to the address issued against the American Board of Missions, by a convention lately held at Syracuse. That address, I doubt not, is capable of most abundant refutation, but I do not conceive that it devolves on me to reply to it. In the details of such a reply, and the numberless questions of fact which it would be necessary to consider, the original question of principle, the question of the relations of Christianity to slavery, the question whether a master of slaves may in any instance be recognized as a Christian, would be quite forgotten.

It is no part of the object, in any of these essays, to *prove* that the slavery which exists in these American States is wrong. To me it seems that the man who needs argument on that point, cannot be argued with.

What elementary idea of right and wrong can that man have? If that form of government, that system of social order is not wrong—if those laws of the southern states, by virtue of which slavery exists there, and is what it is, are not wrong—nothing is wrong. Such a book as Wheeler's " Law of Slavery," leaves no room for any argument to prove that our southern slavery is wrong, if only the reader is gifted with a moral sense. It is, therefore, taken for granted in these essays, from first to last, that every man has rights, and that our American slavery —which denies all rights to some two millions of human beings, and decrees that they shall always be held at the lowest point of degradation—is too palpably wrong to be argued about. The wrong of that slavery, however, is one thing, and the way to rectify that wrong, is another thing. The wrongfulness of that entire body of laws, opinions and practices is one thing ; and the criminality of the individual master, who tries to do right, is another thing. These essays, therefore, treat chiefly of the way in which the wrong can be set right.

New Haven, April 24th, 1846.

CONTENTS.

OCCASIONAL ESSAYS.

SLAVERY.*

[QUARTERLY CHRISTIAN SPECTATOR, 1833.]

THE author of this book is an intelligent and able minister of the gospel, in the Presbyterian Church. A few years ago, he was pastor of a congregation in Prince Edward County, Virginia. Born and educated in that State, and having spent more than forty years there, in the midst of a slaveholding population, he entertained those views of slavery, which, we believe, are common to pious and reflecting men in all parts of the country; he believed in "the moral evil of slavery, and the duty of Christians to let no selfish interest prolong the sin and injustice, but, in the fear of God, to do all they can, in consistency with duty, to fit for and restore to freedom those in bondage." This view led him to favor the Colonization Society, to take up contributions for that object, and to attempt founding an

---

* LETTERS ON SLAVERY : *Addressed to the Cumberland Congregation, Virginia.* By J. D. PAXTON, their former Pastor. LEXINGTON, KY., 1833. 12mo. pp. 207.

2

auxiliary society among his people. Occasionally
he made some little reference to the subject in his
public preaching ; but, as there were usually slaves
in the congregation, and as he knew how readily
some persons might take offence, his allusions to the
" delicate subject," as the Southrons call it, were
few and slight. By marriage he had become the
master of one or two families of slaves. He felt it
to be his duty—and his wife's views were entirely
coincident with his—to make those persons free, as
soon as it could be done with a fair prospect of improving their condition. Accordingly, he says, "we
watched the progress of the Colony at Liberia for
several years ; and, in the mean time, used means
to prepare our slaves for freedom. As soon as we
were satisfied that they had better prospects there of
doing well for themselves, than they could have
with us, we encouraged them to go; gave them such
an outfit as our means afforded, and sent them to the
Colony." These slaves, eleven in number, sailed
from Norfolk, on board the Indian Chief, in Febru-
ary, 1826 ; and were among the first of the slaves
manumitted for the purpose of sending them to Africa.

Not long after the going forth of these freed-men,
and while the excitement, naturally produced in the
neighborhood by such an event, had not yet entirely
subsided, our author commenced a series of essays
on slavery, in the Family Visitor, a religious paper,
which had some circulation among the families of
his charge. The third number of this series contained an energetic exposition of the inconsistency
between slavery, as constituted by the statutes of

Virginia, and the requisitions of the law of love. It gave great offence to those members of the congregation, who had been previously dissatisfied with their pastor's liberating his own slaves; and as Mr. Paxton was well understood to be the author, great efforts were made to create a general disaffection towards him. Immediately on receiving official information that an opposition had been organized against him, he resigned his charge, " leaving the Cumberland congregation to obtain a pastor whose opinions might agree with their own."

Such was the occasion of the letters before us. They were written soon after the author's resignation of his pastoral charge, but have remained unpublished these six years, because the author, unwilling to do anything rashly, yielded to the advice of certain friends, who thought " that on account of existing excitement, some little time should be allowed to pass before they were given to the public." We confess that our judgment differs from that of Mr. Paxton's cautious friends. To us it seems that this little book could have done no great harm, and might have done great good in the six years during which it has been shut up in the author's desk. To us it seems, too, that the excitement of the occasion would have caused the book to be read with interest by many who now may never read it at all.

The first of these letters contains a narrative of facts, relating to the occasion on which the book was written. The second treats of ministerial prudence, and exposes the folly of supposing, that whenever offence is taken at a minister's preaching or conduct, he is of course to be regarded as having

acted imprudently. The third refutes the notion, so
common at the South, that all discussion on such a
subject is to be avoided as dangerous, and shows that
the danger of slavery itself is such as cannot be aug-
mented by temperate and candid discussion. The
fourth exhibits the origin and nature of negro slavery
in the United States, and compares it with the slavery which formerly existed in England. The fifth
shows how slavery violates the principles on which
all our boasted political institutions are founded ;
and inquires what sentence is pronounced upon
it by the law of nature. The five following are an
investigation of the teachings of Scripture in respect
to the morality of slavery. The eleventh and twelfth
exhibit some of the evil tendencies of slavery ; and
argue very strongly that no Christian, of enlightened
views, can lend the sanction of his example to a
system fraught with such tendencies. The thirteenth
refutes some of the arguments most commonly of-
fered in vindication of slavery. The fourteenth and
fifteenth are devoted to the inquiry, " What must
we do with our slaves?" Our author's own example has shown the favorable opinion with which he
regards the efforts of the Colonization Society ; yet,
he is far from thinking, as some seem to think, that
nothing ought to be done except as the emancipated
are carried to Liberia. He proposes several plans
for the removal of the colored population, and obviously regards the separation of the two races as important to the well-being of both ; yet he doubts
whether the removal of all is practicable, and brings
arguments to show that the emancipated slaves
might become, in time, even in the midst of the

country which they now occupy, industrious and happy free laborers. He shows, with much clearness, what can be done by individual slaveholders to promote the general abolition of the system ; and, in the sixteenth letter, concludes with an eloquent array of " motives to immediate effort," drawn from the doctrine of God's retributive dispensations, and from the certainty that dreadful judgments must fall upon a country so laden as ours with the guilt of slavery, unless they are averted by a speedy repentance.

This book is a fair specimen of that sort of discussion on the subject of slavery, which we wish to see more of. The author does not bluster, like some eminent philanthropists in our part of the country ; he does not attempt to mystify and madden the minds of inflammable readers, with the stereotype talk about "immediate abolition ;" he writes like a man who knows whereof he affirms, and who knows precisely what prejudices and errors he has undertaken to combat ; he aims directly at the instruction and conviction of those slaveholders who imagine that there is no wrong in slavery, and that nothing is to be done but to hand down the system, just as it is, to other generations ;—and such is the coolness and clearness, and at the same time the pungency, of his statements and arguments, that slaveholders, meeting with the book, cannot refuse to read, and reading, cannot easily avoid being convinced. We hope the book may have a wide circulation in that part of the country for which it was especially designed. We hope it may be replied to ; and that the author may thus have occasion to come out again, with his strong appeals to undeniable facts and self-evident principles.

In saying all this, however, we do not make ourselves responsible for everything which the author has said. Here and there, if it were worth our while, we might find fault with a position or an argument; but those slips and errors—if they are such—do not affect the great conclusions to which he wishes to conduct his readers. For example: we have our doubts whether the exegesis by which he would get rid of some passages of Scripture often adduced in defence of slavery, is in every instance correct. Yet the general position, that the Bible does not justify or authorize slavery, he defends successfully; for he brings forward the great principles of Christian morality, and applies them to the question in such a manner as leaves no doubt on the mind of the unbiased reader, that, whatever difficulties there may be with the exegesis of particular passages, the Bible is irreconcilably at war with such a constitution of society.

Taking leave, now, of Mr. Paxton and his book, but not of the subject, we propose to occupy a few pages with a scriptural inquiry respecting the morality of slavery.

To many who will read these pages, the question is one of direct practical importance. We have readers, not a few, who are the hereditary masters of bondmen, or who live in the midst of a slaveholding community. And besides these, many of our readers in our own part of the country, will probably be living, by and by, where the laws establish slavery, and where every man, whose circumstances permit

him to employ a servant, is called upon to decide for
himself, whether he will be a slaveholder or not.
Thousands of the natives of the north—young men,
and men more advanced—men in every business
and profession—are continually becoming citizens
of the south, and there find that the question of the
morality of slavery is to them a question personally
and immediately practical.

The subject is important to us all, in another aspect. We at the north, are fellow-citizens with
slaveholders; and between us and them, as fellow-
citizens, there is, and must be, a constant intercourse.
We and they not only meet by our representatives
in the national legislature, but meet personally, both
in our part of the country and in theirs. Many slave-
masters are associated with us, in our various benevolent and Christian enterprises. Often individuals from
among them, brought hither by business, or in pursuit
of health, come and worship with us in our temples,
or as members of sister churches, sit down with us
at the table of the Lord. Not less often, one and
another from among us, finds himself carried by his
business, or is driven by disease, into those parts of
the country where slavery prevails; and there slaveholders not only offer him the civilities of ordinary
hospitality, but, if he is a professor of religion, invite
him to worship with them in their families and in
their temples, and to commune with them in all religious ordinances. Thus, it is an important question to all, how ought we to regard these fellow-
citizens? And this is only another form of the question respecting the morality of slavery. On the one
hand, we are urged to believe that they are without

any responsibility, in relation to the existence and continuance of slavery among them. On the other hand, we are visited by traveling lecturers on slavery, and inundated with pamphlets and papers, urging us to believe that every slave-master is, as such, a criminal of the deepest die, a "felon in heart and deed," whose crime is only inferior " to intentional and malignant murder," a " thief," a " robber," a "tyrant," who deserves to be regarded as the common enemy of the human race. These circumstances certainly give great importance to the inquiry respecting the morality of slavery.

First of all, in this inquiry, it is necessary to define distinctly the subject in debate. *What is slavery ?*

Before attempting a direct answer to this question, it is to be remarked, that there are many varieties of slavery ; that the laws of different countries and ages limit and modify the relation of master and slave, in many different degrees ; and that, therefore, the answer ought to include slavery in all its forms. There may be slavery, where the master has, by the law, an absolute irresponsible power over the persons and lives of his slaves ; and there may be slavery, where the master has no power to put his slave to death, and if he inflicts any punishment beyond a certain measure of severity, he must be called to account at a public tribunal. There may be slavery, where the slave is by the law incapable of acquiring property, incapable of marriage, incapable of testifying in a court of justice, incapable of complaining to a magistrate against the cruelty of his master or of any other person ; and there may be slavery, where the slave is invested with all these rights, and protected in them. There may be slavery, where the slave is allowed to be sold like a horse, at the pleasure or necessity of his master, and to be torn away by force from all the objects of his natural affection ; and there may be slavery, where the slave cannot be transferred from one proprietor to another, except with his own consent. There may be hereditary slavery, entailed upon unborn generations ; and there may be slaves, whose children are free-born. There may be a slavery for life ; and there may be a slavery limited to a term of years. We say, therefore, the definition of slavery ought to include all the varieties of servitude which the word slavery properly denotes, and ought to exclude everything else.

Shall it be said, then, as is often said by those who talk most on this subject, that, for a man to have property in his fellow-men, is slavery? How are we to understand this definition? Has not the master a property in his apprentice—the father in his children—not to say the husband in his wife, and the wife in her husband? Is all the property which one human being may have in another, slavery? Who is he that would abolish slavery, by proclaiming it as an axiom, that it is a crime for one human being to claim property in another? Let him preach that doctrine, if he will be consistent, to his apprentices, or to the apprentices of his neighbor, and exhort them to make the application for themselves. Will it be said, that the master cannot sell his apprentice as the slaveholder can sell his slave? We ask in reply, Is there no slavery where the slave

2*

cannot be transferred from one master to another, without his own consent ? Suppose a law to be enacted, forbidding the master to sell his slave, except with the slave's consent, and making the slave's voluntary signature in the presence of a magistrate essential to the validity of the transfer :—is that the immediate, unconditional, and unqualified abolition of slavery ? Is it said that the master has no property in the person of his apprentice, but only a property in his time and labor, a title to his services ? We ask in reply, Is it necessary to the existence of slavery, that the slaveholder shall have any other kind of property in his slave than what the master mechanic has in his indented apprentice ? Suppose it to be declared by legislation, or by some judicial decision, that the master's property in his slave is simply a property in his time and labor, and not in his blood and bones, and that the slave is only a " person held to service or labor" for his lifetime, and transmitting the same condition to his children :—would that be the immediate and complete abolition of slavery ?

Shall it be said, then, that slavery consists in the obligation to work without wages ? But is not the apprentice bound to work without wages? The apprentice has indeed a compensation for his labor; he does not work for nothing ; he receives, ordinarily, his food and clothing, and he receives instruction in his trade. And so the slave may have a compensation. It is not essential to his condition that he shall work for nothing ; it may be that he has his daily food, his cabin and his clothing ; it is not impossible to imagine that he has food and clothing for his children, and even a shelter and the comforts of animal existence for his aged and disabled parents; nay more, he may be provided with medical attendance in sickness, and with religious instruction on the Sabbath; and the master may regard all this as due to him in consideration of his services; while yet his service is the service of a slave. Will it be said that his compensation is inadequate? We admit it; but are all men slaves who work for an inadequate compensation? In how many parts of the world may men be hired, by thousands, to work for no other compensation than bare shelter and support?

Shall we adopt Paley's definition, that " slavery is an obligation to labor for the benefit of the master, without the contract or consent of the servant?" But may not a man sell himself into slavery? Did not the Hebrew servant, who, at the end of his sixth year of servitude declined the privilege of becoming free, consent and contract to be a slave forever?

We know not how to define slavery more accurately than by saying, It is that *artificial relation, or civil constitution, by which one man is invested with a property in the labor of another, to whom, by virtue of that relation, he owes the duties of protection, support, and government, and who owes him, in return, obedience and submission.* The right which a father has in his children, is a natural right; the relation which involves it, is a relation instituted by the Author of nature. The right which the master has in his apprentice, is the right of the father transferred, within certain limits, and for the convenience and by the consent of the parties, to another person.

But the relation of master and slave has no foundation in nature; it is altogether the work of human legislation. It is a relation entirely artificial; it is an unnatural constitution of society, arbitrarily investing one party with authority and property, and binding the other party to obedient and submissive labor.

Now there are those, we have reason to believe, who think they find in the Scriptures a full justification of slavery; and who bring proof texts to quiet their consciences while they hold their fellow-men, and are resolved to hold them always, in a most degrading bondage. On the other hand, there are men who profess to regard it as one of the plainest points of revelation, that no man can exercise the ownership and government of a slave, in any circumstances for a single hour, without the most atrocious and horrible guilt. The inquiry before us has been undertaken with reference to both these opinions. In pursuing it, then, we are to examine chiefly what light the Scriptures throw on the subject.

A full investigation of the Scriptures in relation to this matter, naturally divides itself into two branches; first, the Mosaic legislation and religion, and secondly, the principles and conduct of Christ and his apostles.

The first point, then, to be examined, is the legislation of Moses on the subject of slavery. Did the great lawgiver of Israel, legislating by Divine inspiration, approve and sanction slavery? If not, did he forbid and abolish it on the plan of immediate abolition? The following positions, we think, will be found too plain to need much illustration, and too well supported to be denied.

1. Moses did not introduce slavery among the Jews. It was even in his time, as it has been ever since, in all the countries of the east, an ancient and established institution, incorporated with all the habits of the people, and with the entire structure of society. As long ago as when Abram and Lot departed out of Haran, about four centuries after the flood, they took with them, not only " the substance which they had gathered," but " the souls which they had gotten in Haran."* The patriarch, sojourning and wandering in the land of promise, was not a solitary traveler; he was respected as the master and proprietor of a body of servants, of whom " three hundred and eighteen " were able to bear arms.† And as to the nature of the servitude of the souls which he had gotten, and the tenure by which they were held, the story of Hagar, the " bondwoman," seems to be a sufficiently palpable illustration.‡ The wealth of Isaac consisted not only in flocks and herds, but in " great store of servants."§ When Jacob returned from Padanaram, his wealth was " oxen and asses, flocks, and men-servants, and women-servants."|| Whether the servants of those days were bought and sold as merchandise, and at what price, let those judge who have read of the sale of Joseph to a caravan of Arab traders—a transaction exactly like what now takes place in Africa, not to say in this country, every day. Such were the ideas and habits of the Hebrews, when Moses undertook to give them laws.

---

* Genesis xii. 5.   † Genesis xiv. 14.
‡ Genesis xvi. 1-9; xxi. 9-11.   § Genesis xxvi. 14.
|| Genesis xxxii. 5.

2. In these circumstances did the inspired legislator peremptorily prohibit slavery? No. He expected that the people for whom he was legislating
would continue to hold bond-servants as property;
and he framed his laws accordingly. Indeed, we
may say, that slavery is as important a title in his
laws, as it is in the statute-book of any State in this
Union. He defines several modes in which persons
might become slaves. (1.) The man convicted of
theft, and unable to make a double or fourfold or
fivefold restoration of the property stolen, was to be
sold to make out the compensation.* (2.) Sometimes a man through poverty sold himself or his
children, or perhaps, was sold, with his family, for
the payment of his debts; a wiser method, surely,
than our Gothic practice of imprisoning the debtor.
This mode of enforcing the payment of debts, was
probably an ancient custom. The legislator takes
it for granted that this will be done, and makes provision for it.† (3.) Captives in war, especially women and children, were held as slaves.‡ (4.) In
connection with a law protecting the Israelite, who
through poverty had sold himself, against the rigor-
ous treatment to which slaves were ordinarily subject, and providing for his emancipation at a fixed
period, it is said, " Both thy bondmen and thy bondmaids which thou shalt have, shall be of the heathen
that are round about you; of them shall ye buy
bondmen and bondmaids : moreover, of the children

---

* Exodus xxii. 1–4.

† Levit. xxv. 39, 47 ; Exod. xxi. 7 ; Nehem. v. 4. 5. See Michaelis
on the laws of Moses, vol. ii. pp. 160–163, 306–308.

‡ Deut. xx. 14

of the strangers that do sojourn among you, of them shall ye buy, and of their families that are with you, which they begat in your land; and they shall be your possession; and ye shall take them as an inheritance for your children after you, to inherit them for a possession."* Such legislation as this, proves beyond debate that Moses did not peremptorily prohibit slavery as a crime. Other particulars are equally remarkable. It is enacted, that if a master should so strike a slave with a rod, as to cause his immediate death, the crime should be punished as murder; but the exception is added—strange, not to say shocking, to our sensibilities—that if the slave survive the injury a day or two, the master's pecuniary loss shall be considered punishment enough, " for he is his money."† The law—of late made so familiar to half the population of this country, by an ingenious temperance tract—which held the owner of a dangerous ox responsible with his life, if through his neglect the ox should cause the death of a man or woman, contains a similar exception. If the ox " has killed a man or a woman,"—" if he have gored a son or daughter," the owner is to be put to death unless his life be redeemed by a sum of money, at the discretion, doubtless, of the magistrate. But, " if the ox shall push a man-servant or maid-servant, he (the owner) shall give to their master thirty shekels of silver."‡ Such a distinction between a

---

* Levit. xxv. 44–46.   † Exod. xxi. 20, 21.
‡ Exod. xxi. 28, 32. See Michaelis on the laws of Moses, vol. iv. p. 260.

freeman and a slave, seems to have been necessary
in making laws for the stiff-necked Israelites; but
our feelings revolt at it.

3. Did Moses sanction slavery? Not at all. He
dealt with it as he dealt with polygamy, with arbitrary divorce, with the levirate law, and with the
old bloody law of the GOEL or blood-avenger. Legislating for a people, in many respects barbarous, and
never remarkably tractable, he wisely considered
what was practicable in such a case, rather than
what was simply desirable. Many were the provisions of the Jewish law, of which Christ might
have said, as he said of that which permitted arbitrary divorces, "Because of the hardness of your
hearts, Moses wrote you this precept." The professed Christian, then, who would set up a justification for slavery, on the ground that the civil laws
of Moses did not peremptorily forbid it, ought to
remember, that, by the same reasoning, he may
justify polygamy, and concubinage, and the divorce
of a wife at the pleasure of her husband. By the
same reasoning, he may make it the duty of the
brother of a deceased husband, to receive as his own
wife the childless widow, for the sake of perpetuating the family and name of the deceased. By the
same reasoning, he may prove that in every case of
homicide, from the most malicious to the most accidental, the nearest relative of the person slain, may
pursue the slayer, guilty or innocent, and may smite
him to death wherever he finds him. The only
question on this point is—Did Moses, with the authority of an inspired legislator, sanction as right,
everything which his code did not prohibit and pun-

ish as criminal? And among Christians, surely, that is no question at all.

4. The Mosaic statutes respecting the relation of master and slave, are obviously modifications and amendments of a previously existing *jus consuetudinarium*,* or common law, and are designed to meliorate the condition of the slave, to protect him from oppression, and to promote the gradual disuse and abolition of slavery. Here, for the benefit of such as have never given their attention distinctly to this point, we will state a few particulars.

(1.) No Hebrew could continue a slave, except by his own free consent, for a longer period than six years; and while he continued such, he was to be treated only as a hireling, whose wages for the six years had been paid in advance. In the year of jubilee, too, every Hebrew who had· fallen into poverty, was to regain his hereditary lands, and was, of course, to go free, that he might take possession of them.†

---

* Michaelis on the laws of Moses, vol. i. pp. 9-15.

† Exod. xxi. 2-6; Deut. xv. 12-18; Levit. xxv. 39-55; Mr. Paxton, pp. 79—84, labors hard to make it out, that these provisions applied to all the slaves which the Israelites were permitted to hold. His argument, in brief, is, that all their slaves were to be circumcised; and that, by being circumcised, they became naturalized in Israel, and were placed on a level with the descendants of Jacob. But was a circumcised slave, therefore, a naturalized Israelite? We answer, No; for Moses has given a particular law of naturalization, Deut. xxiii. 3-9. By that law, it was granted to Edomites and Egyptians, as a peculiar favor, that the grandchildren of such as should settle in Palestine, might "enter into the congregation of the Lord;" and in regard to the Ammonites and Moabites, it is declared, that to the tenth generation, and forever, they should be incapable of becoming Israelites. Yet the Edomites, not to say the Egyptians, were circumcised; and it would seem, that any stranger who desired to eat the passover, might do so

(2.) The master, who in correcting his slave, even with a proper instrument of correction, should cause his immediate or speedy death, was to be punished, as guilty of homicide. Such a law, phrased as it is, cannot easily be understood as anything else than a limitation of the previously allowed power of masters over the persons and lives of their servants.*

(3.) A slave, maimed by his master, was to become free. The language of the law, indeed, includes expressly only two cases of maiming : " If a man smite the eye of his servant, or the eye of his maid, that it perish, he shall let him go free for his eye's sake ; and if he smite out his man-servant's tooth, or his maid-servant's tooth, he shall let him go free for his tooth's sake."† But, as Michaelis has remarked, the lawgiver, by naming the noblest of our organs on the one hand, and on the other, one of those organs that can most easily be dispensed with, and that are naturally lost as old age approaches, plainly intimates that all the other organs are to be considered as included. It is not unfrequently the case in the laws of Moses, that a general principle, instead of being abstractly announced, is inculcated by being involved in two or three particulars.

---

after being circumcised, Exod, xii. 48. So that it is, at least, doubtful whether the circumcision of a slave, and his eating of the passover-feast, was designed to make him a Hebrew, in the sense of the law now in question.

Mr. P. also argues that, at any rate, the foreign slave went out free in the year of jubilee. But the law of the jubilee, which is found in Leviticus xxv., makes a distinction between the foreign servant and the Hebrew, expressly in that particular.—See verses 39–46.

    * Exod. xxi 20.   † Exod. xxi. 26, 27.

(4.) A female slave, in certain cases, became entitled to the privileges of a wife, or in default of these, to her freedom.* The laws here referred to, tended in part to protect the chastity of female servants, and, in part, to increase the number of freeborn children. No master who became a father by his female slave, increased, in that way, the number of persons doomed to bondage.

(5.) The religious institutions of the Jewish nation were, in many respects, calculated to afford relief and privileges to the slave. Being circumcised, he was no longer regarded as a heathen, but was bound to the worship of the God of Israel. The weekly rest of the Sabbath was for him no less than for his master; and the master was expressly enjoined, in reference to this privilege of his servants, to remember the toilsome bondage of Israel in Egypt.† In all the sacred festivals, " the servant and the handmaid " were to partake, no less than " the son and the daughter," and Israel was to remember, " thou wast a bondman."† The tendency of all these things was to create sympathy and kind affection between the master and his servants, and to prepare the latter for the privileges and honors of freemen.

(6.) Kidnapping, or the stealing of men to make them slaves, was punished with death.§ If laws affect public sentiment, then such a law against the crime of reducing men to slavery, was calculated, not only to prevent that particular crime, but also to inspire a horror against slavery itself.

---

* Exod. xxi. 8–11; Deut. xxi. 10–14.   † Deut. v. 14, 15.
‡ Deut. xvi. 11, 12.   § Exod. xxi. 16

(7.) Runaway slaves from a foreign country were not to be given up to their masters, but were to be allowed to dwell in the land, wherever they could find a home.* One effect of this law would be, reciprocal, or rather retaliatory, laws, among the neighboring nations, in regard to fugitive slaves from Palestine; so that, whenever the slave of an Israelite master should find his condition intolerable, a flight of one or two days would almost always carry him to some country from which he could not be reclaimed. Another effect of this law would be to impress strongly on the popular mind, that great truth on which the law is founded, namely, the truth that every man ought to be a freeman.

To all these considerations it is to be added, that the religious teachings and ethical maxims of Moses and the prophets were, in principle and tendency, if not in terms, opposed to slavery. Let it be remembered, that the law of love is the basis of Mosaic, no less than of Christian morality; that it was expressly enjoined on the Hebrews, as a religious duty, to treat strangers and foreigners with kindness;† that God, in his revelations, made himself known to them, especially as the protector of the poor, and the avenger of the oppressed;‡ and that, among the duties most forcibly urged by indignant prophets, in times of sin and judgment, was the duty of letting the oppressed go free, and breaking every yoke;§ and it cannot be doubted, that among the Jews the influence of their religion conspired with the influ-

---

* Deut. xxiii. 15, 16.   † Deut. x. 17-19; Exod. xxii. 21.
‡ Eccle. v. 8; Exod. ii. 23; iii. 9.   § Isaiah, lviii. 6.

ence of their laws, to mitigate the character of slavery, and to promote its gradual extinction.

But, after all, we have exhibited only in part, the tendency of the Mosaic institutions, as it respects slavery. These institutions ought to be considered as a whole, in all their bearings on the increase of a homogeneous Hebrew population; on the industry, and social and moral habits of the people; on their mode of agriculture; on their intercourse with foreign nations; on the augmentation of wealth among them, and its distribution into small estates; in a word, on all their character and condition as a people. This most important branch of the inquiry we can only hint at. He who can examine it in detail, will find, we are sure, that, as these institutions were designed to civilize a rude pastoral people, to fix them on the soil, and form them into a peaceful agricultural community, and gradually to extirpate from among them all those barbarous usages which could not be abolished at a blow; so, in particular, they were fitted to fill the land of Israel with a population who would have no room for foreign slaves, and no use for that kind of "machinery," and whose feelings and habits would be opposed to slavery.

Accordingly, it is worthy of notice, that as Palestine became filled with an industrious and peaceful Jewish population, the practice of employing bond-servants fell into comparative disuse. n the times of our Saviour, we find no very distinct traces of the existence of slavery among the Jews of the holy land. The only "servants" mentioned in the narratives of the four evangelists, except where the word occurs in Christ's parables, are the centurion's

servant miraculously healed,* who was most probably a slave under the Roman law, and the servants
of the high priest's palace,† who may have been
hired servants, but more likely were Jews engaged
for a six years' term of service, according to the Mosaic statute.

What then are the results of our inquiry respecting the legislation of the great author of the Hebrew
polity? Did Moses, legislating for Israel by Divine
authority, approve and sanctify slavery as an institution, or slaveholding as a practice? By no means.
Did he peremptorily forbid and abolish it, on the
plan of immediate abolition? We answer, No; if
he did the Bible is a book past all understanding.

Before proceeding to an examination of the principles and conduct of the apostles in respect to this
subject, we pause, that we may ask our southern
readers to compare their *code noir* with the slave
laws of Moses. Is it not true, without any considerable exception that your laws on the subject
are all designed for the advantage of the master;
to secure him from the loss of his property; to
guard him against insurrection; to strengthen him
in the exercise of a power so absolute, so odious,
that nature stands horror-struck at the bare description; and to fortify the system, as far as possible, against everything that tends to its abolition?
Is not the only considerable limitation of the power
of the master a limitation in the wrong direction—
a limitation against righteousness, against compassion, against religion? Is not almost any cruelty

---

* Matt. viii. 5-13.   † Mark xiv. 65; Luke xxii. 50.

in a slaveholder less offensive—we do not say to
public sentiment, but to the law—than the kindness that would give them their freedom, or that
would even teach them to read the Word of God?
Has not every new law, from year to year, pushed
the same line of policy a little farther? How contrary to all this were the statutes of the great Hebrew lawgiver! His laws affecting the relation of
master and slave are designed, not to afford the
strong new advantages and a more perfect impunity
in oppression, but to relieve the helpless and protect the defenceless; not to construct new entrench-
ments around a barbarous system, at war with
human happiness, but rather to cast down its barriers, and to lay it open to the entrance of improving
and transforming influences. 1687554

At the same time, it may be remarked, that there
is a lesson here for those extra-zealous abolitionists
who permit themselves to be led into denunciations
against the constitution of the United States, and
against the memory of all the framers of that august
compact, on the ground that it does not prohibit
slavery, but allows to slaveholders the power of
representing their bondmen in the national legislature. Undesirable indeed it is, that slavery should
exist under the banner of the great republic;—still
more undesirable that the representatives of slaves
should sit in the capitol; but shall we, therefore,
curse the constitution, and curse the memory of the
men who framed it and consented to it? Is not the
constitution, as it is, the very best that could have
been framed in those circumstances? Is it not far

better than any sane man could hope for, if the
work were now to be done over again? Were not
these undesirable concessions necessary, " because
of the hardness of the hearts" of the people for
whom the constitution was to be framed? It is
well known that the federal compact has been denounced, on this account, by certain agitators, in no
measured terms ; and, unfortunately, certain habits
of reasoning, prevalent in these days, are calculated
to give effect to that sort of denunciation. No matter how much the peaceful and prosperous union of
these states has done for the cause of liberty and
human happiness over all the earth—no matter
what wars and implacable enmities would have
raged perpetually between the rival powers of the
north and south, the east and west, had the plan of
union under one government been permitted to
fail—no matter, though all the blood of the revolution had been in vain, and the enemies of liberal
institutions had found, in the hopeless anarchy of
the American republics an irresistible argument
against popular governments—no matter what destiny would have been entailed on us and our posterity, or what darkness would have settled on all
the hopes of oppressed and fainting nations, had the
convention of 1788 broken up without forming a
constitution, or had the constitution formed been rejected by the people—all these things are not even
the dust of the balance, in the estimation of the
agitators ; all these things are mere matters of " expediency ;" notwithstanding all these things, the
constitution is to be execrated as a compromise with

slaveholders, and an " agreement to act in opposition to the principles of justice."* Let these de-
nouncers be consistent; let them hold up, for the
execration of philanthropists, the concessions to a
hard-hearted and stiff-necked people, which are in-
terwoven with the law given to the Hebrews by the
inspiration of the God of love.

We come now to the second branch of the investigation which we have undertaken. What was
the conduct of Christ and his apostles, in relation to
slavery? Here, as before, we have a twofold inquiry. Did the apostles, in any way, sanction or
justify slavery? If not, did they everywhere preach
to slaveholders, as an essential point of religion, the
duty of instant and unqualified emancipation?

In regard to the conduct of our Saviour, little
need be said ; for, as we have already intimated, it
does not appear that he lived in a slaveholding

---

* We are happy to see that some of the immediate abolitionists, as
they choose to be called, are beginning to take a more rational and more
loyal view of the Federal Constitution. In the recently published " Address of the New York City Anti-Slavery Society"—a pamphlet which,
though written generally in a much better spirit than most of the publications of that school, contains some statements quite too uncandid
to be worthy of refutation—it is stated, with much truth, (1) That the
clause in the Constitution, under which fugitive slaves are reclaimed
from the free States, is necessary to reclaim a runaway apprentice,
and will be indispensable after slavery shall have been abolished.
And (2) that the provision allowing three-fifths of the slaves to be
represented in Congress, is in fact a motive to the abolition of slavery,
inasmuch as the slave States, by abolishing slavery, would be enabled
to represent in Congress five-fifths, instead of three-fifths of their negroes. This is a motive which will one day have a powerful operation. The abolition of slavery throughout the United States would
enable the now slaveholding States to send into Congress, immediately, fifteen or twenty additional representatives.

3

country, and there is nothing in his personal history that can be considered as positively touching the subject. If the centurion's servant, healed by Christ, was a slave, under the Roman law, as we suppose him to have been; and if the Saviour had designed to preach the modern doctrine of immediate emancipation, surely we should find, in connection with the record of the miracle, something on the subject of setting the servant at liberty. If one of our modern abolitionists had been there, among the disciples, the centurion surely would not have escaped without a hot rebuke. But, does all this prove that the Saviour of the world has sanctioned, and acknowledged as right, the practice of holding innocent men in bondage? Because he did not interfere to dissolve the relation of master and servant, in that particular instance, does it follow that he approved of the relation, and that his disciples may buy and sell slaves without fear of offending him, or of dishonoring his gospel? If it is said that this servant was not a slave; we answer, that is a possible case : but if we admit it to be a fact, the admission only removes the incident out of the range of our present inquiry.

In relation to the apostles, the inquiry is not to be so summarily disposed of. As soon as their mission carried them out of Palestine, the moment they entered into any of the great cities of the empire, whether in Syria or Asia, in Greece or Italy—they were in the midst of slavery, rank and flourishing. It is, of course, to be expected that many allusions to slavery will be found in their writings. It is to be expected that on such a subject their opinions will be expressed, and that not indistinctly.

But, here it is proper to inquire, before examining the references to slavery in the apostolic writings, What was the slavery which then existed? Did it resemble at all the negro slavery of modern times? The question is not a difficult one to be answered. Doubtless the laws and usages were various in different parts of the empire, according to the character of the various subject nations, and their ancient civil institutions; doubtless the lot of the slave was less miserable in some provinces than in others; but we presume no scholar will deny that slavery, as it existed at the metropolis, and as it was practiced by Roman citizens, may fairly be taken as a specimen of the slavery which the apostles encountered in their labors, and to which reference is had in their writings.

The following particulars, respecting Roman slavery, are familiar to every schoolboy who has studied Adam's Roman Antiquities.

1. Slaves were held, not as persons, but as things; and were bought and sold like any other merchandise. Fathers might sell their free-born children into slavery.

2. The children of a female slave were the property of her master. There was no regular marriage among slaves; but man and woman lived together by the permission of the master, in a connection altogether like the unlegalized and unprotected marriage of slaves in this country.

3. The power of the master over his slaves was absolute. He might scourge them, or put them to

death,* at his pleasure. The lash was the common instrument of punishment; but sometimes slaves were branded in the forehead; and sometimes they were made to wear a piece of wood, like a yoke, around their necks. Sometimes, too, they were punished by confinement in a workhouse, or house of correction. When slaves were whipped, they were suspended with a weight tied to their feet.

4. If a master was slain at his own house by one of his slaves, or if the murderer was not discovered, all the slaves in his family were liable to be put to death. Tacitus† records a tragedy of this kind, in which a family of four hundred slaves, of whom all but one were probably innocent, were publicly executed. That affair occurred not far from the time when Paul was dwelling in his own hired house at Rome.

5. Slaves could not appear as witnesses in a court of justice. Nor could they inherit anything, or make a will, except with the consent of their masters. In a word, a slave was incapable of possessing property, save as his master gave him the privilege of laying aside a *peculium* from the monthly or daily allowance on which he subsisted, or from the money which he might happen to receive in other ways.

6. Slaves were often treated with great cruelty. Some, indeed, were educated, and employed as clerks, or as teachers of children. Some were the

---

* Pone crucem servo—' Meruit quo crimine servus
   Supplicium? Quis testis adest? Quis detulit?' Audi.
   Nulla unquam de morte hominis cunctatio longa est,
   O demens, ita servus homo est? Nil fecerit, esto.
   Hoc volo, sic jubeo, sit pro ratione voluntas.—Juven. Sat. vi. v. 218.
† Tacit. Annal. xiv. 42, 45.

personal attendants, and humble companions of their masters. Not a few, perhaps, were kindly and affectionately treated ; and were permitted to cherish the hope of becoming free, and sharing in all the immunities and honors of Roman citizenship. But the condition of others, and those not few, was the lowest to which human nature can be degraded. Some served in chains, as the doorkeepers of their masters' houses. Some, in chains, were compelled to dig upon a soil, the fruits of which were never to be their own. Others toiled in subterranean workhouses.

7. The number of slaves was very great. Great the number must have been, when four hundred, the inmates of one house, were publicly butchered, to expiate a single murder. A wealthy Roman was sometimes the proprietor of several thousands.

These particulars, which are only a part of a grammar-schoolboy's learning, are sufficient to show what was understood, in Paul's time, by the words master and servant, and what was then the difference between bond and free. Who will not acknowledge that the state of things in the Roman empire at that time was, at least, almost as bad as the state of things at present in this Federal Republic ? The question is, how did the apostles express themselves, and conduct themselves, in respect to the relation of servitude, as it then existed?

Passing by, as unimportant, all those allusions which merely show the fact, that the first preachers of Christianity had to do with a slaveholding people, we notice, first, Paul's advice to the slaves who were members of the Corinthian Church. "Let

every man abide in the same calling wherein he was
called: [that is, let every man be satisfied to continue in the same social and secular engagements in
which he was when he became a Christian.]   Art
thou called, being a servant? care not for it; but if
thou mayest be made free, use it rather.   For he
that is called in the Lord, being a servant, is the
Lord's freeman ; likewise, also, he that is called,
being free, is Christ's servant.   Ye are bought with
a price ; be not ye the servants of men."*   The
slave is here exhorted to perform the duties of his
station without repining at his lot, inasmuch as bond
and free, who believe in Christ, are alike the servants and the freed-men of the Lord ; and yet, he is
reminded, in language which shows that the apostle
was thinking how God had forbidden the children of
Israel to hold each other in bondage, that if he may
be made free, it is unworthy of his dignity, as the
Lord's redeemed freeman, to be any longer the slave
of a fellow-man.†   Nothing is said, in this epistle,
respecting the duty of masters.   Is it because there
were no masters among the Corinthian Christians?

In addressing the Church at Ephesus, the apostle
exhorts not only slaves but slaveholders.   "Servants, be obedient to them that are your masters according to the flesh, with fear and trembling, [with
the utmost respect,] in singleness of heart, as unto
Christ; not with eye-service, as men-pleasers, but

---

* 1 Cor. vii. 20-23.

† The language of the apostle evidently shows that he was thinking
how God had forbidden the children of Israel to hold each other as
bondmen, Levit. xxv. 42. Mr. Paxton remarks, (p. 122,) that the words
of Paul might well pass for a quotation from Moses.

as the servants of Christ, doing the will of God from
the heart; with good will doing service, as to the
Lord and not to men; knowing, that whatsoever
good thing any man doeth, the same shall he receive
of the Lord, whether he be bond or free. And ye,
masters, do the same things to them, [conduct yourselves towards your servants with the same conscien-
tiousness,] forbearing threatening, knowing that your
Master also is in heaven; neither is there respect of
persons with him."*

A passage, entirely parallel to that just cited, occurs in the Epistle to the Colossians. "Servants,
obey in all things your masters according to the
flesh, not with eye-service, as men-pleasers, but in
singleness of heart, fearing God; and whatever ye
do, do it heartily, as to the Lord and not to men,
knowing that of the Lord ye shall receive the reward of the inheritance, [the wages of future blessedness,] for ye serve the Lord Christ. But he that
doeth wrong, shall receive for the wrong which he
hath done; and there is no respect of persons.
Masters, give to your servants that which is just and
equal, [or equitable,] knowing that ye also have a
Master in heaven."† In both these passages it is
implied, first, that the writer felt slavery to be at best
a hard and painful condition; and, secondly, that in
his view, the idea of a master governing his slaves
conscientiously, equitably, and on Christian principles, was not a contradiction.

It is to be remarked, that one of the bearers of the
epistle last referred to, was Onesimus, a fugitive ser-

---

* Eph. vi. 5-9.   † Col. iii. 22-35; iv. 1.

vant, who, coming to Rome, had been converted under the ministry of Paul, and was now sent back by the apostle to his master Philemon, one of the Colossian Christians. The epistle which the returning fugitive carried to his old master from the imprisoned apostle, cannot but afford some clue to that apostle's views of slavery. " Though I might be much bold in Christ, to enjoin thee that which is convenient, [proper,] yet for love's sake, I rather beseech thee. I beseech thee for my son, Onesimus, whom I have begotten in my bonds; who in time past was to thee unprofitable, but now is profitable to thee and to me : whom I have sent again; thou, therefore, receive him, that is my own bowels. Whom I would have retained with me, that in thy stead he might have ministered to me in the bonds of the gospel, [in my imprisonment for the gospel.] But without thy mind, [consent,] would I do nothing, that thy benefit, [kindness,] should not be as it were of necessity, but willingly. For, perhaps, he therefore departed for a season, that thou shouldst receive him forever ; not now as a servant, but above a servant, a brother beloved, especially to me, but how much more to thee, both in the flesh and in the Lord? If, therefore, thou count me as a partner, receive him as myself. If he hath wronged thee, or oweth thee aught, put that on mine account. I, Paul, have written it with mine own hand, I will repay it."* Onesimus was evidently not of the lowest rank of slaves, but an educated and intelligent man—just such a man as the apostle needed to assist him while

---

* Philem. 10-19.

a prisoner. Paul, sending him back after his conversion, to Philemon, speaks of the new relation of brotherhood which is hereafter to subsist between the master and the servant, and prefers a request for the emancipation of the converted slave, and offers to become responsible for whatever losses Philemon may have sustained by his former unfaithfulness.

Peter, in his epistle to the Christians of "Pontus, Galatia, Cappadocia, Asia and Bithynia," countries, some of which were the Guinea—the very slave-coast*—of the Roman empire, is naturally led to allude to the hard condition of slaves, which he does in language indirectly expressive of much sympathy. The passage need not be quoted. It is of much the same tenor with Paul's exhortations to the same class of Christians.† He enjoins it upon them, by Christian motives, to be conscientiously obedient and respectful towards their masters, and to submit patiently to the unkindest treatment.

This kind of preaching to slaves is, in Paul's epistles to Titus and Timothy, made a part of the duty of Christian ministers. To Timothy it is said, "Let as

---

* 'Cappadocian,' was with the Romans another name for slave. Cicero says of one of his enemies, ' *Cappadocem modo abreptum de grege venalium diceres* '—an expression nearly equivalent with the phrase sometimes used at the South, ' He is as stupid as a new negro.' It is remarkable that Juvenal, alluding to the degradation of society, occasioned by the honors and privileges bestowed on emancipated slaves, enumerates, as the native provinces of those slaves converted into knights, the same countries mentioned by Peter in the inscription of his epistle, with the exception of Pontus.

Faciant equites Asiani,
Quanquam et Cappadoces faciant equitesque Bithyni,
Altera quos nudo traducit Gallia talo.—*Sat.* vii. 14.

† 1 Pet. ii. 18-21.

3*

many *servants as are under the yoke*, count their own
masters worthy of all honor, that the name of God
and his doctrine be not blasphemed. And they that
have *believing masters*, let them not despise them,
because they are brethren ; but rather do them service, because they are faithful and beloved, partakers
of the benefit. These things teach and exhort. *If
any man teach otherwise*, and consent not to whole-
some words, the words of our Lord Jesus Christ, and
to the doctrine which is according to godliness, he is
proud, knowing nothing, doting [diseased] about
questions and strifes of words, whereof cometh envy,
strife, railing, evil surmisings, etc.—*from such withdraw thyself*."* Here we see, *first*, that there were
bond-servants among the Christians in the region
where Timothy, as an evangelist, was to superin-
tend the organization of churches, and was to put
in operation the entire system of apostolic institutions ; *secondly*, that some of those bondmen had
masters who were recognized as believers ; *thirdly*,
that even at that early period, there were some who
undertook to infer from the gospel the abolition of
slavery as a civil institution ; and *fourthly*, that Paul
advised Timothy to have no partnership with such
teachers.

The reader has now before him a full view of
what the apostles have said respecting slavery, and
the duties of master and slave. So far as our present inquiry is concerned, the whole may be summed up in the following remarks :

1. The apostles have said nothing in vindication

---

* 1 Tim. vi. 1-5; Titus ii. 9, 10.

of slavery. In all the allusions of the New Testament writers to this subject, not a word is found which seems as if they approved of one man's holding another in bondage; not a word to encourage the master in perpetuating the degraded condition of his servants; not a word to caution him against the "mistaken philanthropy" of giving them their freedom.

2. It is manifest that the apostles regarded the condition of slaves with compassionate sympathy. Their language, when they inculcate on servants the duties of their station, breathes always the spirit of condolence. They enjoin it on every slave who may be made free, to accept the higher responsibilities of a freeman, as more worthy of one redeemed by the blood of Christ. We find in their writings no pictures of the happiness of servitude; none of the sickening common-places of southern philanthropy about the contentment of slaves, their exemption from care, the lightness of their tasks, and the superiority of their condition over that of a free peasantry. Every word in the New Testament, that touches on slavery, is in a very different tone.

3. Immediate emancipation on the part of slaveholders, was not a condition of membership in the apostolic churches. Philemon, a man of consideration among the saints at Colosse, was a slaveholder. Paul expected that Timothy, in fulfilling his office of an evangelist, would have occasion to exhort some slaves, at least, that had believing masters, (πιστους δεσποτας.) In the church at Ephesus, as well as in that of the Colossians, there were so many masters, that it seemed proper to address them as a distinct

class. All these men must have been acknowledged as credible professors of Christianity. Yet, not one word is said by way of enjoining upon them the immediate emancipation of their servants; not one word which implies that to live in the relation of a master, even for an hour, is to live in high-handed iniquity ; not one word which intimates any sympathy with a certain Address to the Presbyterian Church, which has been widely circulated at the expense, we presume, of some of the leading abolitionists, (so called,) in the city of New York. " Slaveholding," says that address, "under every possible modification, is man-stealing. Man-stealing, as combining impiety in principle, falsehood in claim, injustice and cruelty without intermission and without end, is the most flagrant iniquity which a sinner can perpetrate. All profession of religion, by a man who thus acts, is a gross deception." Such is the modern doctrine of immediate emancipation. The master of a slave, *under every possible modification* of that relation, is guilty of the most flagrant iniquity possible ; his crime is one in which impiety and falsehood, injustice and cruelty unremitting and interminable, are all combined ; and if he attempts to make a profession of religion, he is a gross deceiver. Such were the πιστοι δεσποται of whom Paul speaks to Timothy. Such was Philemon, whom the great apostle styled, "our dearly beloved, and fellow-laborer." Such were the "masters" in the churches at Ephesus and Colosse. The apostles did not teach immediate abolitionism, nor did they form their churches on that basis.

4. The apostles seem to have taken it for granted,

that the Christian master would do for his slaves all that was consistent with their welfare and the public good. So Paul acted in the case of Philemon and Onesimus. The slave is sent back to his master, and the master's legal claim is distinctly recognized. Yet it is taken for granted, that Philemon will act with other views than a regard to his own pecuniary interest; that he will look on Onesimus not as an article of merchandise, but as a man, a brother, and will treat him accordingly. It is taken for granted that now, since the grace of God has taken effect on the once unprofitable slave, and has fitted him to be happy and useful under the responsibilities of freedom, his Christian master will not only forgive his past offences, but will send him forth free, to be the helper of Paul, or in any other way to advance the kingdom of the Saviour. So to masters generally, the command was, ' Render to your servants that which is right and equitable ;' and it was left to an enlightened conscience to decide, in each instance, what the principles of right and equity required. Of course it was taken for granted, that the slave would be treated as an intelligent and immortal being ; and that, whenever the great rule of equity, the golden rule of love, required the slave to be put upon his own resources, and set to act under his own guidance, he would be emancipated.

We find the discussion extending itself beyond our expectation, and the printer warns us to bring it to a conclusion. Let us look, then, at some points of Christian duty in regard to slavery, as we have to do with it in this country at the present day.

1. Ought the naked fact, that a certain man is the master of slaves, to exclude him, without farther inquiry, from the communion of the churches? We answer, No. It may be that he came into that relation without any act of his own. It may be that he is doing for the welfare of those slaves, conscientiously and diligently, the most that existing circumstances will allow. It may be that if he emancipates them from under his hand, the sheriff will immediately arrest them, and sell them to the highest bidder. It may be that he is prosecuting a course of measures, which, after less than a seven years' " apprenticeship," will result in their real emancipation. The mere fact that he is invested with a certain legal power over the persons of these individuals, implying a certain legal title to their services, is not necessarily a crime. The author of these letters on slavery, while he was educating his servants to take care of themselves, and providing their outfit to Liberia, was not a criminal, though he was still their master, and as such, responsible for their good government. The question, in each individual instance, is, Whence did this man obtain his power over these his fellow-men? and to what ends is he employing it? On the answer to this question will depend the propriety of allowing his claims to be considered as a servant of Christ. If he makes it a business to breed slaves for market— if he treats rational and immortal beings only as if they were cattle—nay, if he does not see carefully, not only that their physical wants are supplied, but that they are restrained from vice, and properly instructed, especially in the things of their everlasting

peace ; and if, after due admonition, he will not repent of his iniquity, then treat him as a heathen man and a publican.

2. Ought the mere buying of a slave to exclude the buyer from Christian communion ? Not the mere act of buying. The question is, To what end, and with what views, was the purchase made ? A friend of ours in the District of Columbia, once bought a negro woman with a family of children. ' Away with him !' cry the abolitionists—' Excommunicate him !' But, " good friends, sweet friends, let us not stir you up to such a sudden rage ;"— take your fingers from your ears, and hear the story. That woman and her children were for sale, and, by the operation of the internal (or, as the word is sometimes spelled, not incorrectly, infernal) slave-trade, were about to be transported to the extreme south. There are philanthropists who would have stood by to witness the transaction, and would have eased their burthened minds, by letting off a volley of execrations. But our friend has taken no degrees in their college. Though not worth a dollar beyond his daily earnings, he bought the whole family, borrowed the money on his own responsibility, with the endorsement of a friend, and, if we mistake not, owes for it, and pays seven per cent. interest for it, to this day. Those slaves are now free, not in Liberia, but in America ; and their benefactor, a standing mark for the obloquy of some who think themselves the only abolitionists, toils on in the great cause of suffering humanity, burthened with the debt of that purchase. When any of those who have arrayed themselves as his enemies, shall

have been guilty of a similar imprudence, we will
give them credit for being warm-hearted as well as
hot-headed. But to the question, Shall this man,
for buying slaves, be excluded from the communion
of the saints? Often may we commune with him
in Christian ordinances here; and be it ours to sit
down with him at the "marriage-supper of the
Lamb."

Take another case. Suppose some wealthy individual undertakes to demonstrate, by a public experiment, the practicability and good economy of
converting slaves into free laborers. He purchases
a tract of land in Florida, where no State government can forbid philanthropy to exert itself, but the
laws and liberties of the Union are his protection.
Next, he goes into the slave-markets of Virginia,
and buys fifty or a hundred slaves. These he trans-
ports to his new plantation; as their legal master,
invested with all the powers of government over
them, he establishes such regulations as he deems
necessary to their order, their industry, their improvement, and sets them at work, intending to make
them, as fast as they will indemnify him for the expense of the undertaking, the free proprietors of the
soil on which they labor. Shall such a man be excommunicated for buying slaves? We earnestly
wish that some of the gentlemen who are expending
thousands of dollars in a conscientious, (we dare
say,) but still most unprofitable crusade against
African colonization, might be induced to divert a
part of that expenditure to buy slaves for such an
experiment.

These cases are stated for the sake of showing that

the crime does not consist in the act of buying, but in the purposes and views with which the purchase is made. The man who, born free and among the free, makes himself a slaveholder for the sake of gain; (shame to New England that there are so many such,) the man who buys his fellow men, as he would buy oxen, simply with a view to his own interest, that he may have them to sell again if he can sell them at a bargain, or that he may enrich himself by their reluctant toil, and when he has done with them, leave them to 'heirs he knows not who;' the man who buys slaves with any other design than to do them all the good he can, is most manifestly an offender against the law of love, and ought to be dealt with as such, by all the churches. He is not only guilty of wrong towards the individuals whom he purchases, but he gives the full support of his example to the entire system of slavery, and voluntarily makes himself a partaker in all the sins which that system, by its natural tendency, diffuses through society.

3. What ought the slaveholder to do? What ought he to do in regard to his own slaves? Obviously, he ought to do for them just what, on a careful consideration of their character and all their circumstances, he sees will be most for their good ; we do not speak here of the public good, because *their* good and the *public* good are, in reference to this question, inseparable. Let him consider, not only their actual condition, but their liabilities. Be it that their master is kind and attentive to all their wants ; be it that they are well governed, and supplied with religious instruction ; be it even that they

are contented with their present lot, and are unwilling to change places with the free blacks around them ; all this weighs but little in the scale against their liabilities. They are liable, as chattels, to be attached and sold for their master's debts ; and, whatever commercial revolution, whatever accident, involves him in pecuniary embarrassment, is likely to bring on them a distress, compared with which bankruptcy and poverty are nothing. So, on the death of their master, when his estate comes to be settled and divided, they are liable to the same fate ; all their connexions may be sundered; and, torn from all that is home to them, they may be consigned to a condition the more terrible for the former alleviations of their lot. What, then, does a wise regard for their welfare—what does imperative justice towards them—demand of their master? Ought he not, if possible, and as soon as possible, to secure them against such contingencies? Against such contingencies they cannot be secured, as the laws now are, but by being made free. Does he ask, How can I make them free? We answer, You can educate them for liberty ; and, as fast as they become at all competent to take care of themselves, you can put them in the way of earning a passage to Africa, or let them choose their own course to whatever country will open its doors to receive them.

But what ought the slaveholder to do in regard to the system of slavery? First of all, he ought, on every fit occasion, to bear his testimony against it, and against the legislation which creates and supports it. He ought to declare himself, fearlessly, the enemy of slavery, and the friend of whatever will mitigate the curse, or promote its peaceful abolition. Where such an evil pervades society, offending the heavens with its atrocity, and cursing the very soil with its afflictive influences, if any individual has a right to be silent, that individual is not the slaveholder. His silence respecting such an evil, is approbation ; his neutrality, is partisanship. The timidity which seals his lips, makes him, in fact, an abettor and supporter of all those laws, the mere digest of which is enough to make the brow of an American crimson with shame. If all those men in the southern States, who are, in conscience and in judgment, dissatisfied with slavery—who are convinced that it must be abolished, and desire to see that consummation peacefully accomplished—would but speak out like freemen, there would soon be in those States such a demonstration of public opinion, as would make the advocates of slavery cower and hide their heads for shame.

Yet, in order that the slaveholder's testimony against slavery may be complete and effectual, his example must accord with it. If, on his own plantation, he perpetuates the system just as he received it from his predecessors ; if his slaves, born, living, dying, in the lowest condition to which humanity can be degraded, transmit that condition unmitigated to their children ; if he does not set himself in earnest, and like a working-man, to the work of elevating and blessing those whose destiny is committed to his hands—no matter what opinions he may express hostile to the system—the testimony of his example is recorded for slavery, slavery as it is, slavery forever. The man who emancipates his slaves, and places them where they will be free indeed, whether in Liberia or in Hayti, whether in the British West Indies or on the prairies of Illinois, bears a testimony against slavery, which the consciences of his neighbors cannot resist, and which he may think of with pleasure on his dying bed.

THE ABOLITION OF SLAVERY.*

[QUARTERLY CHRISTIAN SPECTATOR, 1833.]

IT cannot be doubted, that much of the dispute which exists at the present time among those who are seeking the extinction of slavery, is to be ascribed to some mutual misunderstanding in regard to the import of terms. One class of philanthropists, among whom the author of this book has recently become a standard-bearer, insist on what they call the immediate, unqualified, complete abolition of slavery. Another class, whose philanthropy is equally unquestionable, think that though the immediate and universal emancipation of two millions of slaves may be better than the perpetuity of slavery, a progressive and gradual subversion of the fabric of society now existing in the southern States would be much more desirable, as respects the well-being of both the slaves and their masters, and as respects all those great interests of the human race, which are confessedly involved in the result. Between these two classes—strange to tell—has arisen contention, such as turns the very temple of our reli-

---

* LECTURES ON SLAVERY AND ITS REMEDY. By AMOS A. PHELPS, Pastor of Pine street Church, Boston. Published by the New England Slavery Society, 1834. 18mo. pp. 284.

gious anniversaries into a scene of clamor and violence.

We set up no claim to be considered peculiarly disinterested or impartial in this controversy. It is not for us to pretend to act as umpires. Our readers all know, that our sympathies are neither with the advocates and apologists of slavery, nor with the crusaders for immediate and universal emancipation. We have taken our ground with that class of Christian philanthropists, who, reasoning not from the abstract equality of all men, as to political rights, but from the great law of love, believe, first, that abolition in almost any form, is better than perpetual and immitigable slavery; and secondly, that the immediate emancipation of two millions of slaves in the United States, would be far less beneficent, and therefore far less equitable towards the slaves themselves—whose interests and rights in the matter are first to be consulted—than some more progressive change of their relations to the other classes of society. Yet, unless we deceive ourselves, we are not committed on this subject, so as to be unwilling to learn. The subject has been much in our thoughts for years; and as we are sure, that we understand it now better than when we began to study it, so we confidently expect to learn more and more in years to come. Our discussions of this subject, as of every other, are pursued, we trust, for truth rather than for victory. And though we may be sometimes excited—unduly excited, perhaps, by the treatment we receive from men of whom we have a right to expect, if not the courteous bearing of gentlemen, that Christian candor and kindness which is far better—we still hope, that no personal feelings of ours will lead us to pervert clear testimony, or will hinder us from acknowledging the force of argument.

The first thing necessary to the adjustment of the controversy, between the two parties of those who cherish a common enmity against slavery, is, that we have a distinct and right understanding of the terms ' abolition' and ' emancipation,' as they are used in this controversy. . It is common with immediate abolitionists, in their arguments on the subject, to describe in the strongest terms, some of the horrors of that slavery which exists in the southern States ; to deal out certain aphorisms about inalienable rights; and to infer, that every slave in the United States ought to be emancipated instantaneously, and that all slavery ought to be instantaneously abolished. What do they mean? is the first question. Do they make a right use of language ? is another question.

To take an example—the authenticity of which will not be called in question—the ' National Anti-Slavery Convention,' in their declaration of principles, argue as follows :—

' Those, for whose emancipation we are striving—constituting at the present time at least one-sixth part of our countrymen— are recognized by the law, and treated by their fellow-beings as marketable commodities—as goods and chattels—as brute beasts; are plundered daily of the fruits of their toil without redress; really enjoying no constitutional nor legal protection from licentious and murderous outrages upon their persons ; are ruthlessly torn asunder—the tender babe from the arms of its frantic mother—the heart-broken wife from her weeping husband—at the caprice or pleasure of irresponsible tyrants. For the crime of having a dark complexion, they suffer the pangs of hunger, the infliction of stripes, and the ignominy of brutal servitude. They are kept in heathenish darkness, by laws expressly enacted to make their instruction a criminal offence.   *   *   *

No man has a right to enslave or imbrute his brother—to hold or acknowledge him, for one moment, as a piece of merchandise —to keep back his hire by fraud—or to brutalize his mind by denying him the means of intellectual, social, and moral improvement.

The right to enjoy liberty is unalienable. To invade it, is to usurp the prerogative of Jehovah. Every man has a right to his own body—to the products of his own labor—to the protection of law—and to the common advantages of society. It is piracy to buy or steal a native African, and subject him to servitude. Surely the sin is as great to enslave an *American* as an *African.*

Therefore we believe and affirm—That there is no difference, *in principle*, between the African slave-trade and American slavery ;

That every American citizen, who retains a human being in involuntary bondage as his property, is, according to scripture, a *man-stealer ;*

That the slave ought instantly to be set free, and brought under the protection of law ;   *   *   *   *   *   *

That all those laws which are now in force, admitting the right of slavery, are therefore before God utterly null and void ; being an usurpation of the Divine prerogative, a daring infringement on the law of nature, a base overthrow of the very foundations of the social compact, a complete extinction of all the relations, endearments, and obligations of mankind, and a presumptuous transgression of all the Holy Commandments—and that therefore they ought to be instantly abrogated.'

We quote this passage, not to argue with it, but to inquire, What do these people mean by immediate emancipation ? Take the first paragraph, on which, if we mistake not, the whole argument was supposed by the signers of that address, to depend. That paragraph seems to be the definition of that state of things which ought to be immediately abolished—the description of that slavery from which the slaves ought to be immediately delivered. Suppose, then, the abolition of that state of things to have taken place. Suppose the slaves to have been actually delivered from the wrongs above recited. What is the change? The slaves are no longer 'recognized by the law, or treated by their fellow-beings, as marketable commodities, as goods and chattels, as brute beasts;' they are henceforth "PERSONS *held to service.*" They are no longer 'plundered of the fruits of their toil;' the law takes care effectually that they shall have such guardianship, support, and comfort, as shall be a full equivalent for their labor. They are no longer 'destitute of constitutional and legal protection from licentious and murderous outrages on their persons;' the law, through the ministration of courts and officers instituted for the purpose, guards them, as effectually as other subjects of the law are guarded against violence and abuse. They are no longer 'ruthlessly torn asunder—the babe from its mother, the wife from her husband—at the caprice or pleasure of irresponsible tyrants;' it is provided by law, that every master shall be held *responsible* for all his treatment of his servants—that families of slaves shall not be separated without their own consent—and that no slave shall be transferred from one master to another, without his own voluntary subscription (if he be an adult, or the subscription of his parents, if he be an infant,) to the instrument of transfer. They no longer 'suffer the pangs of hunger, the infliction of stripes, and the ignominy of

4

brutal servitude, simply for the crime of having a dark complexion;' they are well fed; their rations are forfeited only by the apostolic rule, as a punishment for indolence; stripes are inflicted on them only for evil-doing, at the sentence of a magistrate, or if you please, other more civilized penalties have superseded the infliction of stripes; their servitude has ceased to be brutal. They are no longer " kept in heathenish darkness, by laws expressly enacted to make their instruction a criminal offence;"—the face of legislation has been turned the other way; strong and thorough enactments have provided for their instruction at the public expense; and the master, whose slaves are found untaught, is held guilty of a crime against the prosperity and safety of the State. Suppose all this to be a reality. Is this what is meant by emancipation, immediate and complete? Is this the instant and unqualified abolition of slavery? Tell us not, that this must of course result in sweeping away the last vestiges of servitude. The question is not, what will it grow to—but what is it? Is it immediate abolition—instantaneous, universal emancipation?

We answer, No. Emancipation—abolition, means more than all this. All this may be, while yet the slaves have not begun to be their own masters. There is no emancipation till the slave is made a free man. All short of this, is the improvement of his condition, the alleviation of his bondage. To say, that the slave is "brought under the protection of the law," is something short of saying, that he is " instantly set free." To make the slave an apprentice for life, or for a term of years, or for a single

year; to establish, that he is not a chattel, but a
person; to secure for him an equitable compensation
for his toil; to protect him against abuse; to legal-
ize and guard his domestic relations; to provide
for his moral and religious instruction, and for the
education of his children, is not of course to make
him instantaneously a free man. All this is not all
that the convention mean by emancipation, when
they get among their abstractions. There they demand for the slave, not merely a legal personality,
not merely protection, compensation for labor, domestic rights, and the means of instruction; but
liberty—inalienable liberty—liberty which is his already, and always has been, save as he has been
and is precluded from the enjoyment of it by " laws
which before God are utterly null and void." Do
they understand the extent of their demand? Do
they intend to denounce, as an " usurpation of the
prerogative of Jehovah," any law which, regarding the slave as a minor, an infant, incompetent
for the present to control himself, should provide
employment for him, and forbid him to stroll away
from it—should declare him incapable of making
contracts, except under the direction and advice of
his conservator—should regulate the application and
expenditure of his earnings, and should make arrangements for his being "gradually" introduced
into the privilege of self-employment, of self-control, and of disposing of his own earnings at his
own pleasure? Is the immediate emancipation for
which they contend, the emancipation inferable
from their abstract principles? Or is it merely the

abolition of those particulars enumerated in their description of slavery ?

We have before us, in the " Preamble and Constitution of the Anti-Slavery Society of Lane Seminary," the following " exposition of immediate emancipation," given for the very purpose of " preventing misapprehensions." " It has been extensively adopted," say the writers of that document, " as expressing the views of abolitionists, and embodies substantially our own." We doubt not, that it was intended to express fearlessly all that they mean, and all that they do not mean, by immediate emancipation :—

' " By immediate emancipation, we do not mean that the slaves shall be turned loose upon the nation, to roam as vagabonds and aliens—nor

That they shall be instantly invested with *all* political rights and privileges—nor

That they shall be expelled from their native land to a foreign clime, as the price and condition of their freedom.

But we *do* mean—that instead of being under the unlimited control of a few irresponsible masters, they shall really receive the protection of law ;

That the power which is invested in every slaveholder, to rob them of their just dues, to drive them into the field like beasts, to lacerate their bodies, to sell the husband from his wife, the wife from her husband, and children from their parents, shall instantly cease ;

That the slaves shall be employed as free laborers, fairly compensated and protected in their earnings ;

That they shall be placed under a benevolent or disinterested supervision, which shall secure to them the right to obtain secular and religious knowledge, to worship God according to the dictates of their consciences, and to seek an intellectual and moral equality with the whites." '

In this definition, or, as the young men of the Lane Seminary choose to call it, this " exposition of immediate emancipation," the only particular which implies emancipation at all, in the sense of investing the slaves with freedom, is the demand, " that the slaves shall be employed as free laborers." That expression, taken by itself, might be understood to mean, that they are to be immediately free to labor or not to labor at their pleasure, free to find employment for themselves according to their liking, and free to dispose of their earnings according to their own discretion. But against such a construction, the writers seem to have guarded at the outset, by saying, " We do not mean, that the slaves shall be turned loose upon the nation, to roam as vagabonds and aliens." In other words, they do not mean, that the slaves are to be immediately invested with SELF-CONTROL.

This, if we understand the meaning of words, is not immediate emancipation. The slave, we repeat, is not emancipated, till he becomes a free man. You may make the master responsible, and limit his power. You may take the slave out of the power of his master entirely, and put him under an overseer appointed by the public. You may do for his physical comfort, for his protection, for his instruction, whatever seems needful. But he is not emancipated, till he goes forth, like the freed apprentice at the expiration of his indentures, his own master, " loose to roam" whithersoever he pleases.

No man can tell what abolition is, till he can first tell what slavery is. The immediate abolition of slavery, is the immediate annihilation of that state

of things which the word slavery denotes. Mr.
Phelps, in the book before us, is the first immediate
abolitionist whom we remember to have met with,
who was not too immediate—in too much haste for
abolition, to undertake a distinct definition of the
thing to be abolished. " Slavery," he tells us, " is
an assumed right of property in man; or, it is the
principle, admitted in theory, and acted on in practice, that in some cases, each individual being his
own judge in the case, it is lawful to hold property
in man." He accompanies this definition with
several pages of explanation, from which we learn,
that, in his view, wherever a man holds his fellow-
man as property, as not a person but a thing, ' such
as an ox or a horse,' there is slavery, and there
only. It would be unfair, after his explanations, to
infer from the expression, " property *in* man," that
he condemns as slaveholding, the legal property of
the master in the time, strength, and skill, acquired
or acquirable, of his apprentice. By " holding
property in man," he means simply, " holding man
as property"—simply holding and treating a rational
and accountable creature of God, a brother of the
human family, as a thing without rights, a mere
article of merchandise. The thing, then, which is
to be immediately abolished, and the extinction of
which is all that is necessarily meant by immediate
abolition, if Mr. Phelps' definition of slavery is a
true one, is nothing else than the practice of owning men, or rather of assuming and claiming to own
them, as chattels.

This definition of slavery is a very compendious
method of proving, that the relation of the slave-

holder to his slaves is invariably, simply, and inex-
cusably sinful. Our objection to it is, that it is not
a definition of all servitude, but only of that servitude which implies sin on the part of the master.
It was obviously framed with a view to the propo-
sition—All slaveholding is criminal. It was framed
by a mind desirous of giving to its own positions a
fair aspect, at least, of reason and consistency, and
seeking a basis on which to construct the doctrine
of immediate emancipation—a doctrine that shall
make every master of slaves, in all conceivable circumstances, and without any possibility of explanation or defence, an oppressor, a man-stealer, a pirate,
an enemy of the human race. If we understand
the meaning of terms, a man may be constituted by
law the master of slaves, and may exercise over
them all the duties of guardianship and government,
without considering them or treating them as property, and may yet be a slaveholder—the master of
slaves, in the common acceptation of those terms
among all who speak the English language. Those
slaves are slaves, so long as they are not emanci
pated. They are not emancipated, as common
sense understands emancipation, till they cease to
be under the control and guardianship of another.

Mr. Phelps' definition of emancipation corre-
sponds, as we might expect, with his definition of
slavery. In answer to the question, " What does
your immediate emancipation mean ?" he says :—

' It is simply, that the slaves be at once delivered from the
control of arbitrary and irresponsible power, and, like other men,
put under the control of equitable laws, equitably administered.
Slavery, as I have shown, is the principle, that man, in some

cases, at his own discretion, may hold his fellow-man as property. This, adopted as a *practical principle*, is slavery; rejected as a *practical principle*, is slavery rejected. Immediate Emancipation, then, means that slaveholders, as individuals, and as a community, should at once give up this as a principle of action, and so doing, give up all that treatment which is based upon it, and thus put their slaves on the footing of men, and under the control of motive and law. It is, for example, that England should at once yield the *principle* of taxing us at pleasure, without our consent; and in this *one* act yield, of course, all the treatment growing out of, and based upon that principle.

Or more specifically, immediate emancipation means.

1. That the slaveholder, so far as he is concerned, should cease at once to hold or employ human beings as property.

2. That he should put them at once, in his regard and treatment of them, on the footing of men, possessing the inalienable rights of man.

3. That instead of turning them adrift on society, uncared for, he should offer to employ them as free hired laborers, giving them, however, liberty of choice, whether to remain in his service or not :*

4. That from this *starting point—this emancipation from slavery itself*, he should at once *begin* to make amends for the past, by entering heartily on the work of qualifying them for, and elevating them to all the privileges and blessings of freedom and

---

* Suppose some of them are children, without parents, boys at fifteen years of age. *Ought* he to give *them* that "liberty of choice?" Suppose one of them, at the age of thirty, is but a boy of larger growth, as ignorant, as unfitted to employ himself, as incompetent to take care of and use his own earnings, as a child. Ought he to give to such a one that liberty of choice? Again, what does that liberty of choice amount to, as the laws are in the Southern States? To what but a free choice between going forth and being arrested and sold by the sheriff, on the one hand, and on the other hand, a continuance under the government and protection of his old master? Not to leave an unfair impression respecting Mr. Phelps' meaning, we add, that he himself says, on the preceding page, " We would not turn the slaves adrift on society, if we could. So far from it, we are opposed to such a measure. We insist, even, that THE MASTER HAS NO RIGHT THUS TO SET THEM AFLOAT ON SOCIETY, unlooked after and uncared for."

religion ;—thus doing what he can to emancipate them from their ignorance, degradation, &c.—in other words, from the *consequences* of slavery, as well as from the thing itself.

Thus much in respect to the individual. In respect to the community, as such, the scheme means,

1. That, in its collective capacity, it should yield the principle of property in man, and thus cease to recognize any human being as the property of another.

2. That, by wise and equitable enactments, suited to the various circumstances of the various classes of its members, it should recognize them, all alike, as men—as subjects of equal law, under its, and only its, control, to be deprived of ' life, liberty and the pursuit of happiness,' on no account but that of crime, and then, by due and equitable process of law.

And farther, in respect to those slaves who might be disposed to leave their master's service, and become idle vagrants in society, the scheme means,

1. That they should come under the control of vagrant laws— just as white vagrants do.

2. That, if they commit crimes, they should be tried and condemned like other criminals, by due process of law.'

We understand by abolition, much that is not included in Mr. Phelps' description of it. Slavery, according to our definition, is *that artificial relation, or civil institution, by which one man is invested with a property in the labor of another, to whom, by virtue of that relation, he owes the duties of protection, support and government, and who owes him, in return, obedience and submission.* Our notion of the abolition of slavery, is the ENTIRE DESTRUCTION of that artificial constitution of society, which takes away from one man the power of self-control, and puts him under the protection and control of another. The immediate emancipation of a slave by his master, is the instantaneous dissolution of the relation

4*

in that individual instance. The immediate abolition of slavery, in a state or country, is the instantaneous dissolution of that relation between all the
masters and all the slaves, by some sudden violence,
or by some act of legislation. While the slave is
passing through a period of pupilage, controlled by
the discretion of another, his emancipation may be
in progress, but it is not complete. While the slaves
of a country are considered by the law as not yet
fully competent to the responsibility of directing their
own movements and employments, so long—though
the process of abolition may be going forward with
great rapidity, and though the result may be as sure
as the progress of time, and though the statute-book
may have fixed the date at which the slaves shall
be left to their own discretion—slavery is not completely abolished.

In taking our stand, then, against immediate
emancipation, as the duty of the individual master,
and against immediate abolition as the duty of the
Legislature, we do not oppose what Mr. Phelps, and
men like him, of logical and calculating minds, argue for, under those names. As for the *thing* which
alone they profess to *recognize* as slavery, we hold
it to be invariably sinful. As for the thing, which,
when they attempt to speak accurately, they call
emancipation, we hold it to be the plainest and first
duty of every master. As for the thing, which they
describe as the meaning of immediate abolition, we
hold it to be, not only practicable and safe, but the
very first thing to be done for the safety of a slaveholding country. The immediate abolition against
which we protest, as perilous to the Commonwealth

and unjust to the slaves, is a different thing from that which the immediate abolitionists think they are urging on the country.

Why, then, dispute about words? Why not let these men state their object, and call it by what name they choose? We answer, because words in such a case are not mere breath, but things, and things of great importance in their effect on the public mind, and in their effect on those who use them. "In questions of philosophy or divinity, that have occupied the learned, and been the subject of many successive controversies, for one instance of mere logomachy," says Coleridge, " I could bring ten instances of *logodædaly*, or verbal legerdemain, which have perilously confirmed prejudices, and withstood the advancement of truth, in consequence of the neglect of verbal debate, that is, the strict discussion of terms." This sagacious remark is, at least, as true respecting questions of political right, and of practical morality, as it is respecting questions of abstract philosophy, or scientific theology. In the present instance, it is not mere logomachy to dissent strongly from these immediate abolitionists ; there is, in their use of terms, a certain logical sleight-of-hand, which perplexes, irritates and inflames the public, and the influence of which on their own minds, combining with the exciting character of the subject, and with the peculiar temperament of some among their leaders, tends to embitter their philanthropy, and to turn their sense of right into something too much like rancor.

The sophism by which they unwittingly impose on their own minds, and inflame the minds of others, is this: the terms "slavery," "slaveholding," "immediate emancipation," &c., having one meaning in their definitions, and, to a great and unavoidable extent, another meaning in their denunciations and popular harangues. Thus they define a slaveholder to be one who claims and treats his fellow-men as property—as things—as destitute of all personal rights; one, in a word, whose criminality is self-evident. But the moment they begin to speak of slaveholders in the way of declamation, the word, which they have strained from its proper import, springs back to its position, and denotes any man who stands in the relation of overseer and governor to those whom the law has constituted slaves; and consequently every man who, in the meaning of the laws, or in the meaning of common parlance, is a slaveholder, is denounced, with unmeasured expressions of abhorrence and hate, as an enemy of the species. What is the effect of this on their own minds? What —on the minds of those who happen, from one cause or another, to be ripe for factious and fanatical excitement against the south? What—on the minds of those who, without unraveling the sophistry of the case, know that many a slaveholder is conscientious, and does regard his slaves as brethren? What —on the minds of those slaveholders themselves, who are conscious of no such criminality? So of immediate emancipation. They define that to be an immediate cessation from the sin of claiming and treating men as chattels; but when they begin to urge this duty, in appeals to popular feeling, the phrase "immediate emancipation," cannot be hindered from meaning an immediate discharge of the slave from all special guardianship and government, and his immediate investiture with the power of self-control. This, they are understood to mean by the great mass of those who hear them, and this they do actually imply in many of their appeals, notwithstanding their definitions and restrictions. And what is the effect? The public understands them as demanding immediate and complete emancipation, in the obvious meaning of the terms; and the public at large, north and south, east and west, denounces them as visionary and reckless agitators. Hence it is, that even in those States where the hatred of slavery is most pervading and most intense, the call for an immediate abolition meeting, is so often the signal for some demonstration of popular indignation. What is the effect on themselves? Convinced, as they are, by their definition, of the self-evident duty of immediate emancipation, as they define it, and of the indispensable necessity of that emancipation, as preliminary to any other effort for the benefit of the slaves, they forget that immediate emancipation, in the ordinary acceptation of terms, is not equally a self-evident duty, and equally indispensable, as preliminary to other efforts; and so they look with contempt, with dislike, and, unless they are very watchful over their own spirits, with something akin to malignity, on the efforts now made at the south, by Christians of various denominations, for the thorough religious instruction of those held in bondage. They "must husband their strength." They "have no energies to waste in the chase of phantoms." They "cannot afford to be diverted from the main object by eloquent speeches, and touching appeals, about plans of instruction." They declare, peremptorily, that "all attempts at instruction are a real evil." Those attempts may, indeed, inform the mind of the slave with "truths which are essential to his salvation," but still they are to be deprecated as "*a real evil*," inasmuch as slavery without instruction is so much more fertile in horrors, wherewithal to garnish the appeals of abolitionists, and to rouse the public mind to action. If such a man as Mr. Phelps, (see p. 111 of the work before us,) a minister of the gospel, with a mind gifted by nature, and disciplined by education, can be deluded by this "verbal legerdemain" into the expression of such sentiments, what may we not expect from men of a lower order as to intellect and spirit.

We say, then, we cannot consent to be enrolled among the doctors or disciples in this school of immediate abolition. Though their immediate abolition may be a harmless thing, as they define it, they insist on arming that harmless thing with a most harmful name. Their well-intended definitions, unable to overcome that intrinsic power by which words retain their popular signification, define only to mystify, and mystify only to irritate.

We know it is often said, that any doctrine short of immediate emancipation, puts the conscience of the slaveholder asleep, and justifies him in transmitting slavery unmitigated to another generation. But nothing can be more unwarranted than such an assertion. The duty of *immediate emancipation* is one thing. The *immediate duty* of emancipation is another thing. That duty, the present duty of beginning the emancipation of his slaves, the instant duty of

commencing a process with them, which shall infallibly result in their complete liberation, at the earliest
date consistent with their well-being, may be urged
at once on every slaveholder as a direct and indis-
putable corollary from the great law of love. Such a
process, under whatever form it may be commenced,
must imply at the outset, that, in the estimation of the
master at least, the slave is no longer a chattel, but
a person; no longer a thing, but a man, invested
with the majesty of God's image, and endowed with
the rights that belong to God's intelligent and accountable creature.

Here, then, let the public sentiment of the country
speak out for the emancipation of slaves, and for the
abolition of slavery. This is the gradual abolition
which we stand ready always to advocate, without
the liability to mean one thing when we define it,
and another thing when we urge it. Let it be everywhere insisted on, as the first point to be carried,
that to hold men as property, to claim them, and use
them, and dispose of them, as things without personality, and without rights, is a sin, with which neither
humanity nor religion can have any compromise.
On this point, the north can be made to speak through
all the organs of public sentiment, as with the voice
of many thunders. On this point, the feeling in
the free states is unanimous, and has been for these
forty years. The preachers of immediate abolition
often profess, that a great battle must be fought, before even New England will come out against slavery. A battle must be fought, indeed, before New
England will fall in with their measures, or adopt
their style; but it is nothing better than a libel on

New England, to affirm, that there is here one particle of sympathy with slavery, or any feeling adverse to its abolition. Where, in New England, can even the repulsive power of immediate abolitionism drive New England men from their avowed abhorrence of slavery, in all its forms and operations? Nothing is wanting but the occasion and call, to bring out the public sentiment of all the north in one loud cry of reprobation against the practice of making merchandise of men.

Nor will it be found impracticable to discuss this point at the south, or to convince even slaveholders of the wrong of claiming their slaves as 'property, in the same sense with their brood mares.'* It is not impracticable; for there are hundreds of masters there, who are convinced already, and who act on the conviction, that they stand to their slaves, not in the relation of ownership over property, but in the relation of guardianship and government over men, intelligent, and invested by the God of nature with the rights of humanity, yet ignorant, dependent, and, but for the master, defenceless. By the power, not indeed of heat, and smoke, and fury, but of light and love, that conviction may be made to spread, till, having first pervaded the churches there of every denomination, it shall become the strong conviction of the popular mind; and till the majesty of the people, speaking by distinct enactments, shall pronounce that the slaves are persons, having human rights, and, as such, subject to the law, and

---

* It seems incredible that such a comparison should have been made by an advocate of slavery, within a few months past, in the Legislature of proud Virginia. Yet such is the fact.

under its protection. Then will the keystone of the mighty fabric of oppression have been taken away; and legislation will have begun, effectually, the abolition of slavery.

We appeal, therefore, earnestly, to all the rational philanthropists of the so-called Anti-Slavery party, to cease from the bewildering cry for an *immediate* emancipation, which, as defined by them, is either not immediate, or not emancipation; and for an *immediate* abolition, which, as they explain it, is to leave slavery mitigated, indeed, but not yet abolished. We call on them to forsake all fraternity with those who insist on thus blinding themselves, and abusing the public. We call on them henceforth to use language in its proper acceptation; and when they mean to demand that men shall no longer be held and treated as merchandise, to demand it only in terms that shall convey their meaning clearly to every mind. Let them go with this point to the General Assembly, and all the Synods of the Presbyterian Church, to the General Associations of New England, to the Conferences of Methodism, to every assembly and convention by which public sentiment, on a point of morals, can be directed, or through which such sentiment can find fit utterance. Let them persuade every ecclesiastical tribunal in the land, to fix it as a principle, that he who buys, or sells, or treats, his fellow-men as merchandise, is to be dealt with as a sinner. We will go with them; our voice shall be lifted up as loud in the demand as theirs. Let them employ the press in all its forms of influence, till first the buying and selling, and then the owning and treating of men as merchandise, shall

be infamous throughout the land. We will be their
hearty coadjutors. It needs no long-continued effort—it needs only wise and vigorous effort—to make
the traffic in human beings, and the claim on which
that traffic rests, infamous, utterly infamous, even
among slaveholders. Make that traffic infamous;
waken the public conscience at the south, to decide
upon it as it is; and then the spirit, first of individual emancipation, next of general abolition, will
come in like a resistless flood. What is that which,
at the present time, stands more than anything else
in the way of abolition? It is the domestic slave-
trade. It is the fact that slaves have a market price,
and can be exchanged for money, at the pleasure or
necessity of the proprietor. The market for slaves,
in the recently settled cotton and sugar States, is the
only cause which makes the slaves of Maryland and
Virginia, of Kentucky and Tennessee, worth holding as property. The value of slaves in Maryland,
depends entirely on their value at New Orleans.
Shut up the southern market, and the Maryland
slaveholder is richer without his slaves than with
them, so that his pecuniary interest is on the side of
emancipation. Make him feel that he has no right
to sell his slaves—make him see that he cannot sell
them without infamy—and to him the market is
shut up already; nothing but benevolence can hinder him from the most immediate emancipation, unless the laws forbid him.

We are confident that the appeal which we here
make to rational abolitionists, will not be in vain.
We entreat them in behalf of our common country,
and in behalf of all those interests of mankind, which

depend on the internal peace and continued prosperity of this nation; we entreat them in behalf of the slaves, the objects of their sympathy; we entreat them as men of soberness and reason, as friends of man, as friends of Him who came to preach deliverance to the captives—we beg them not to reject this appeal, without a candid and serious consideration.

PRESENT STATE

OF

THE SLAVERY QUESTION. *

[QUARTERLY CHRISTIAN SPECTATOR, 1836.]

THIS little book will do more for its author's reputation, with that portion of mankind whose favorable opinion is most to be desired, than any other
one thing which has come from his pen. We have
read it with almost unmingled satisfaction. The
chapter of "explanations," that on the "evils of
slavery," that on the "means of removing slavery,"
and the short concluding chapter on the "duties of
the free States," are the best parts of a book in
which almost every page is very good. A fine and
lofty moral spirit breathes through the whole. The
only portion which betrays at all the habits of the
Unitarian theologian, is the chapter in refutation of
"the argument which the Scriptures are thought to
furnish in favor of slavery." Not that there is
Unitarianism in that chapter; indeed the whole
book is orthodox in its air and spirit; and there are
passages which, read with evangelical views, and
construed as an evangelical reader would construe

---

* SLAVERY. By WILLIAM E. CHANNING. Boston: 1835.

them, have a higher meaning, and a still greater cogency, than they could have had in the mind of their eloquent author. The seven pages in which the Scriptural argument is dispatched, betray the Unitarian only as they show that Dr. Channing is in the habit of reasoning from what he conceives to be the genius of Christianity, rather than from the inspired record of what Christianity is.

Dr. Channing's ground is, briefly, that so far as slavery divests its victims of all personal rights ; so far as it reduces human beings to the rank and condition of cattle; so far, in a word, as it converts men into property, it is sin, simple, unqualified sin. He discriminates justly between the wrong of slavery, that is, the wrongfulness of those laws which make the negro a chattel, and refuse to recognize him in any other relation—and the guilt attached to the individual, who, not seeing how to lay down the authority committed to him by those laws, exercises that authority, not for his own emolument, but for the welfare of his servants. Upon those masters who hold the slave " not for his own good or for the safety of the State, but with precisely the same views with which they hold a laboring horse, that is, for the profit they can wring from him," he pours a torrent of eloquent indignation ; while he freely acknowledges, that all masters are not thus guilty. In regard to the means of removing slavery, he holds, that the best, safest, happiest remedy, is in the hands of the masters; that the institution of new relations between the master and the servant, without the master's full consent, though it may be far better than the perpetuity of the relations now exist-

ing, cannot but be attended with disaster; that
while the recognition of the slave as a man entitled
to the benefits of good government ought to be immediate, his *emancipation* must be a gradual process ; that the slave ought to be trained for self-support, by being taught to labor under the impulse of
other and manlier motives than the mere terror of
the lash, by seeing new privileges and honorable
distinctions awarded to the honest and industrious ;
by being made to feel, that he has a family whose
happiness depends on his industry, integrity and
prudence, and by being imbued with the truths and
motives of the Gospel of Christ. We need not say
how entirely these views coincide with our own.

One chapter is devoted to abolitionism in the now
technical meaning of that word. The author, while
exhibiting his objections to the spirit and proceedings of the anti-slavery societies, vindicates them
from the charge of *designing* to promote insurrection among the slaves, and denounces with great
solemnity and earnestness the parricidal attempts
that have been made to suppress their proceedings
by violence. His greatest objection seems to be
against the system of *agitation*, by which the anti-
slavery men have sought to compass their ends. Of
this system of agitation he says :

'From the beginning it created alarm in the considerate, and
strengthened the sympathies of the free States with the slaveholder. It made converts of a few individuals, but alienated
multitudes. Its influence at the south has been evil without
mixture. It has stirred up bitter passions and a fierce fanaticism,
which have shut every ear and every heart against its arguments
and persuasions. These effects are the more to be deplored, be-

cause the hope of freedom to the slave lies chiefly in the disposition of his master. The abolitionist proposed, indeed, to convert
the slaveholders ; and for this end he approached them with vitu-
peration and exhausted on them the vocabulary of abuse! And
he has reaped as he sowed. His vehement pleadings for the
slaves have been answered by wilder ones from the slaveholder ;
and, what is worse, deliberate defences of slavery have been sent
forth, in the spirit of the dark ages, and in defiance of the moral
convictions and feelings of the Christian and civilized world.
Thus, with good purposes, nothing seems to have been gained.
Perhaps (though I am anxious to repel the thought) something has
been lost to the cause of freedom and humanity.'—pp. 141, 142.

On this text we offer a few comments, illustrating
the recent history and present bearings of the slavery
question in this country. What Dr. Channing says,
is for the most part truly said, and well said ; yet
in some points it is far from being the whole truth.

The system of agitation pursued by the abolitionists has " strengthened the sympathies of the free
States with the slaveholder." True ; yet this increased sympathy with slaveholders, is not produced
by the system of agitation alone. It is by their
schemes of agitation, taken in connection with their
doctrine of *immediate* freedom, and their usurpation
and perversion of the name of abolitionist, that the
anti-slavery societies have produced in the free States
so considerable a reaction favorable to slavery. Dr.
Channing finds himself compelled, by the persecu-
tions and the mobs which have been got up against
these societies, to take sides with a party whose doctrine of immediate emancipation he renounces, whose
system of agitation he deprecates, and whose spirit
of denunciation he abhors. Just so, thousands of

the best of men, struck with the ferocity of the denunciations indiscriminately launched against all
slaveholders in all possible circumstances, have been
constrained to take sides with slaveholders, and to
say, whatever may be true of slavery, slaveholding
is not necessarily so bad as you represent it. Those
who have demurred at the new doctrine of immediate
emancipation, or its corollaries—such as the exclusion of every slave-owner from all Christian communion, have been vilified in the publications of these
reformers, as "dough-faces," "pro-slavery advocates," "apologists for oppression and man-stealing;" and by suffering the same reproaches with
the slaveholder from the same quarter, have been
compelled thus far to sympathize with him. The
name of abolitionist, which justly belongs, as a name
of honor, to all those States which have provided for
the extinction of slavery within their own territory,
and to every citizen of those States who approves
and honors such a policy, has been perverted and
degraded by being claimed as the distinctive name
of a bitter, contentious, and therefore obnoxious party; till many who once would have gloried in such
a name, and who, when it shall have regained its
legitimate meaning, will glory in it again, having
lost their sympathy with the name, have uncon-
sciously become less interested in the thing. Under
such influences, it is not strange that there has been
a temporary reaction in the public sentiment of the
free States; nor is it strange, that political editors
and others at the north, presuming on the force and
permanancy of this reaction, and having an object

to gain, have even ventured to defend the whole
theory and practice of slavery and the slave-trade,
as they exist in the southern States.

At the south, this system of agitation "has stirred
up bitter passions and a fierce fanaticism, which have
shut every ear and every heart against its arguments
and persuasions." So says Dr. Channing, and we
cannot deny that it is so. Yet if any suppose, that
the furious fanaticism of southern demagogues has
all been created by the anti-slavery societies, they
entirely misunderstand the matter. The direct influence of the immediate abolitionists has been far
less at the south; their publications have had a far
more limited circulation there, than is implied in
such a supposition. Besides, others who discussed
the subject of slavery before the modern doctrine of
immediate emancipation was broached, before the
present system of agitation was dreamed of, found,
as Dr. Channing has found since the publication of
this book, that it is not the doctrine of immediate
abolition only, nor the scheme of northern agitation
only, nor a fierce denunciatory temper only, nor the
combination of all these things only, that is odious
at the south; but that every discussion of slavery in
whatever quarter, and in whatever form; every proposal for the abolition of slavery, whatever the spirit
in which it may be conceived, and whatever the arguments by which it may be enforced, is sure, if only
it'attracts attention at the south, to be met with a
growl of fanatical defiance.

As we understand the matter, the most important
effect of the anti-slavery agitation thus far, has been
its influence on the feelings, opinions, and party

5

sympathies of that small portion of the southern community which was predisposed to favor the abolition of slavery. The great majority of active ministers of the gospel at the south, seeing, as they were compelled to see, the disastrous obstacles which slavery rears in the way of the gospel, by its influence on the master, on the slave, on the form and spirit of society; very many of the more devoted and intelligent members of the various Christian churches, becoming gradually more and more associated with the churches of the free States in philanthropic and Christian enterprises, and continually receiving religious intelligence and religious papers and books from the north; many thinking and sober men, considering the subject in the light of politics and political economy, and imbued with the free spirit which breathes through all modern literature; were not only ashamed of slavery, but were ready to receive more light on the question of its moral character, and to ask, how can it be abolished?—These classes generally have been somewhat acquainted with the movements of the immediate abolitionists, and have read enough of their publications to know something of their doctrines, their proposals and their spirit. On these persons, the influence of the anti-slavery societies has indeed been "evil without mixture." The idea of immediate and unqualified emancipation they could not entertain for a moment. Moved by their abhorrence of a doctrine which seemed to them so extravagant; by an excusable indignation at the denunciations hurled against them and their fellow-citizens; by the fear of being thought to entertain some sympathy with "the fanatics of the north;"

and by the natural yielding of each individual mind
to the current of public sentiment; they have taken
sides with the most thorough defenders of slavery,
and to some extent, with the most fanatical denounc-
ers of the liberty of speech and thought.   Thus it is,
that while a spirit as malignant as ever thirsted for
blood, has blazed over the southern States, there has
hardly been in all the south, one whisper of protes-
tation.   Such is the triumph of the anti-slavery societies.   They have silenced, they have annihilated
for the time, that party in the southern States which
was opposed to slavery, at least, in theory, and
which was inclined to promote inquiry respecting a
safe and righteous abolition.

But what is the cause of that excitement of "bitter
passions and fierce fanaticism" which is now raging
at the south?   We have already intimated, that the
cause is not to be found in the operations of our anti-
slavery friends; and we know it will be put to us to
say, Whence all this excitement?   Whence these
outrageous proceedings?   Whence the before unheard of claim, that Congress has no power to make
laws for the protection of the "inalienable rights" of
some five or six thousand persons under its "exclusive jurisdiction" in the District of Columbia?
Whence the demands, so fatal to liberty, that the
right of petitioning Congress shall be trampled under foot, and peaceful and respectful petitioners
treated with insult by the national legislature; that
the entire post-office establishment shall become a
literary inquisition; that the free States shall make
laws to abridge the freedom of the press, the freedom
of the pulpit, the freedom of voluntary association?

Whence the preposterous claim, that in a country where no other subject is too high or sacred for discussion; where the atheist may assail Christianity with ribaldry in taverns and steamboats; where agrarians may hold public meetings to discuss and plan the philanthropic scheme of abolishing property; where a brazen-fronted woman may lecture in the theatres against the slavish institution of marriage; free men in the free States shall not speak, nay, shall not think, on the subject of slavery? To us, the cause of all this mad excitement seems to lie quite on the surface of passing events. When were the votes of the south given to make a northern man President of the United States? When was there any danger of their being thus given, till the canvassing for the now coming election was commenced.

We will speak more distinctly. Was it not quite certain, some two or three years ago, in consequence of the overwhelming influence and popularity of the present administration, that unless some desperate experiment should be made upon the public mind, many southern votes, not to say a great majority of the southern votes for the presidency, would be given to a citizen of the north? Is it not notorious, that at that time a newspaper in the city of Washington, representing and leading a certain party in the southern States, began in concert with associated presses still farther south, to address the fears, prejudices and pride of the slaveholding States, on this very subject of northern interference with slavery? Was it not a manifest and leading object of the appeal then commenced, to make the question of slavery entirely a political question with every southern man? And can there be any doubt that this was done—this excitement kindled, this agitation kept up, month after month—simply with a view to revive and aggravate that intense sectional feeling which heretofore has always been strong enough to direct the votes of southern men? What is it that is going on in Congress at this very time, in relation to the anti-slavery memorials? Are not the southern leaders continually urging their extravagant demands with a view to compel the friends of that northern candidate either to take some position that shall ruin their candidate at the south, or to make some cowardly and servile concession that shall disgrace him at the north? How are the people continually abused by the demagogues of all parties, who play upon their ignorance, their prejudices, their basest passsions, to gain the power or the emoluments of office!

Of all parties, we say—What more affecting illustration of the degradation of the political press can be demanded, than the fact that at the north, while partisans of the administration have attempted to throw upon their opponents the odium of an alliance with the anti-slavery societies, the equally unprincipled attempt has been made on the other side, and has been persevered in with infinite effrontery by journals of great authority and wide circulation, to fix the same odium on the friends of the administration?

In our judgment, then, the immediate abolitionists are only to a limited extent responsible for the excitement in the slaveholding States. They have been the occasion rather than the cause or source of the mischief. Political men, having political ends in view, have taken advantage of their ill-advised operations, to blow the unquenchable fanaticism of the south into a devouring flame.

Another unfortunate result ascribed to the system of agitation pursued by the anti-slavery societies, is, that " deliberate defences of slavery have been sent forth in the spirit of the dark ages, and in defiance of the moral convictions and feelings of the civilized world." These defences of slavery, the atrocity of which surpasses even Dr. Channing's power of expression, are to be traced, we apprehend, to several causes, among which the anti-slavery agitation is by no means the most considerable.

No man has forgotten, that in the summer of 1831 there was an insurrection of slaves in Southampton County, Virginia, in the sudden fury of which some sixty or seventy white people were murdered. The eyes of the southern people were opened for a moment to the horrors of that condition of society in which they live. In Virginia, particularly, it was felt that something must be done ; and when the Legislature of that great State met, in the winter following, memorials were presented, praying that measures might be taken for the abolition of slavery. At once it appeared, that in the Legislature of old Virginia there was a powerful abolition party. The whole subject of slavery—its injustice, its impolicy, its perils, the practicability of its removal—all was discussed with open doors, in the presence of crowded and excited auditories ; and speeches, worthy of the best days of Virginian eloquence, were reported for the newspapers, and were scattered over all the

south, to be read in every family. The session closed
without any decisive action on the subject ; yet not
without the expectation, that in the progress of another year some plan would be matured which should
secure the removal of slavery from that commonwealth which gave birth to Washington, and the soil
of which is hallowed by the ashes of the father of
his country.

In this emergency, it became necessary that something should be done to convince the people of Virginia of the safety, the profitableness, the republican-
ism, and the respectability of slavery. Not a little
was done by speeches in the capitol, and by essays
in the newspapers; but the champion of slavery,
who appeared just in time to turn the tide of public
opinion, was one " Thomas R. Dew, Professor of
History, Metaphysics and Political Law, in William
and Mary College." This gentleman, whose name
we trust will be duly honored by posterity, was the
author of an article on the debate in the Virginia
Legislature, which having been first published, with
much curtailment, in the American Quarterly Review, was soon afterwards published entire at Richmond, forming a pamphlet of one hundred and
thirty-three large pages. We have read the pamphlet diligently, and with no little admiration. The
learned professor of history, metaphysics and political
law, " boldly grapples with the abolitionists on the
great question." He argues, that the practice of
enslaving captives taken in war is the first step which
marks the departure of mankind from primeval barbarism ; and that inasmuch as it is perfectly just for
two nations or tribes, in a state of mutual hostility,

to kill each other to the greatest possible extent, the men, women and children who, instead of being murdered outright, are reduced to perpetual and absolute slavery, have nothing to complain of, but everything to be thankful for. He argues further, that where all the property is in the hands of a particular class, or where the government through weakness or inefficiency fails to afford protection, there the holders of property will be the masters, and the others will necessarily, and therefore of course righteously, be held as slaves. Not stopping even here, he urges the argument, that in many barbarous or overcrowded countries people are reduced to such extremity of suffering, that they will consent to be slaves for the sake of having a slave's food and raiment, and, in some savage tribes, " a father will sell his son for a knife or a hatchet." And lest any doubt should remain in respect to the perfect equity of absolute and hereditary slavery, such as exists in Virginia, the striking and conclusive position is taken that " all governments, even those of the States of our confederacy, have ever been considered as perfectly justifiable in enslaving for crime." All this he considers as proving that " slavery is the necessary result of the laws of mind and matter;" and hence he infers, " that it was intended by our Creator for some useful purpose." Proceeding to set forth the advantages which have resulted to the world from slavery, he insists that this benignant institution, which by some unaccountable fatality is everywhere spoken against, " has been perhaps the principal means for impelling forward the civilization of mankind." In particular, he shows by the conjoined

light of history, metaphysics and political economy,
that it diminishes the frequency and the horrors of
war; that it makes the migratory man domestic,
and the indolent man industrious, and should have
been seasonably applied to save the Pequots, the
Mohawks and the Cherokees from extinction; *and*
that it raises woman (listen, O ye fanatics, and be
forever silent) from the condition of a mere beast of
burden to her proper station, and endows her with
graces and accomplishments. The African slave-
trade next comes under consideration; and here the
ingenious author seems to think, with Sir Roger De
Coverly, that "much may be said on both sides;"
though, as the revival of that trade, under the sanction of the laws, would seriously interfere with the
profits of the Virginia slave-breeders, he is on the
whole not disposed to reverse the judgment which
the conscience of the civilized world has pronounced
upon this traffic. Next he undertakes to expose the
futility of all possible plans for the abolition of
slavery. Through this part of his book, which is
by far the most considerable in extent and in ability,
we have no time to trace the progress of his argument. One or two points, however, in that argument,
must be mentioned, to illustrate the *cold-bloodedness*
with which the subject is treated. He shows that in
Virginia the slaves are worth in market one hundred
millions of dollars; and he infers that this property,
being nearly one-third of all the property existing in
that great State, would be annihilated by *any* scheme
of abolition, leaving Virginia a desert. He shows
that negro slaves are the great staple of Virginia,
inasmuch as "upwards of six thousand are yearly

5*

exported to other States," so that the chivalrous commonwealth of Virginia receives from the sale of human beings, born under its own motto of *sic semper tyrannis*, not less than $1,200,000 every year. In the professor's own words: "Virginia is in fact a negro-raising State for other States. She produces enough for her own supply, and six thousand for sale." He shows, furthermore, that so long as the planters of the more southern States can buy negroes from abroad at a cheaper rate than the cost of raising them at home, so long comparatively few slaves will be raised on those plantations; and so long the slave-holders in Virginia will be able to realize their millions by the exportation of negroes. " The slaves in Virginia," he says, " multiply more rapidly than in most of the southern States; the Virginians can raise cheaper than they can buy; in fact, it is one of their greatest sources of profit." He brings his work to a conclusion, by considering distinctly the alleged injustice and evils of slavery : and in refutation of the vulgar errors on this subject, he maintains that slavery is not wrong in the abstract; that its moral effects are not pernicious, but, on the contrary, the more absolute the slavery the more magnanimous will be the master, and the more contented and happy will be the slave; that slavery is a powerful promoter of the spirit of liberty; that there is no danger from plots and insurrections, but the more numerous and compact the population the greater the safety; and finally, that the notorious and lamented decay of old Virginia is owing not to slavery, but to "the exactions of the federal government."

This pamphlet—to the ability of which our rapid

sketch has by no means done justice, for arguments
in support of slavery must needs suffer by being condensed—produced a powerful impression upon the
State of Virginia.   Nor can it be considered strange
that such was the fact.   Professor Dew himself remembered, and inadvertently quoted, as a great
truth, the saying of Hobbes, " that men might easily
be brought to deny that things equal to the same
thing are equal to each other, if their fancied interests were opposed in any way to the admission of
this axiom."   It was easy then to make the people
of Virginia believe, that while their slaves were worth
one hundred millions of dollars, and while the ex-
portation of a part of the annual increase was bringing into the State one million two hundred thousand
dollars yearly, slavery could not be so bad a thing
as it had seemed, under the excitement which followed the Southampton massacre.   Accordingly,
when the Legislature came together again, and a
whole year had passed without another insurrection,
there seemed to be no occasion for any farther discussion, and Professor Dew's book was thenceforth
considered to be perfectly unanswerable.

Since that time defences of slavery have been
multiplied at the south.   Formerly, southern men
were generally in the habit of acknowledging that
slavery is in some sense an evil, and excused it by
pleading the difficulties in the way of abolition.   But
now they as generally take the ground that the state
of society in which the working-class are held as
slaves is the very *beau ideal* of a well-regulated community; that this institution is the nurse of patriot-
ism, of refinement, of all heroic and generous senti-

ments ; an excellent promoter of good morals, of public tranquillity and domestic happiness ; and that all the religion which does not teach that God made negroes on purpose to be slaves, is sheer fanaticism. All the unqualified and shameless defences of slavery that have been uttered at the south since 1832, seem to us to have been derived directly or indirectly from the great repository of doctrines and arguments found in Professor Dew's " Review of the Debate in the Virginia Legislature." And that which first put the southern orators and essay writers upon this barbarian defence of one of the most barbarous institutions on earth, was not the anti-slavery agitation at the north, but rather that agitation so much nearer the seat of the evil, which ensued upon the Southampton massacre, and which, for one whole winter, thundered in the capitol at Richmond.

Undoubtedly this now prevalent practice of defending slavery in the abstract, has been promoted, as Dr. Chaaning intimates, by the measures of the anti-slavery societies. Yet it is not to be imagined that such arguments are designed exclusively or chiefly for northern readers. The design is to operate upon the southern public, to put down entirely those ideas of the insecurity, the impolicy, and the injustice of slavery, which so lately threatened the oldest and greatest of the slave States with abolition, and to aid in those political agitations to which we have already referred.

" Perhaps something has been lost to the cause of freedom and humanity." Certainly the good cause has lost ground within the last four years. Yet we enjoy the consolation of believing, that the evils

which Dr. Channing deplores, and which are indeed
to be lamented as great evils, will be only temporary,
and under the benignant providence of Him who can
make the wrath of man to praise him, will be, in
the end, productive of good. It is not to be expected
that public sentiment, in respect to a subject so involved with innumerable interests, and entangled
with all the complications of prejudice and passion,
can be reformed in the southern States, without continued conflicts, and the liability to frequent reaction.
Such a reaction we are just now witnessing. But
that reaction will react again. Every high-wrought
excitement, especially every excitement got up by
extra agitation, is essentially transitory. And when
the hour of this present excitement in the south shall
have passed, there will be found men at the south,
who will dare to think for themselves, and who, not
having the fear of Lynch-law before their eyes, will
dare to say, that an arrangement which puts one-
half of the population of a State under the most absolute despotism, leaving them without any legal
protection for one of the rights of their human nature, and which does all that can be done to hinder
them from outgrowing their original barbarism, or
becoming in any manner capable of freedom, is neither safe, nor politic, nor just. In other words, discussion, debate, free inquiry on the subject of slavery,
now suppressed everywhere beyond the Potomac,
will break out again. None can tell how near the
occasion is, that shall put a new aspect upon all
these discussions. Another massacre like that of
Southampton might not do it. The burning of a city
might not do it. But a reduction of the prices of

cotton and sugar some twenty-five per cent., for two successive seasons, would operate resistlessly to enlighten public sentiment in all the slaveholding States; and at whatever time such an event may take place, the men will be found who, in the name of the commonwealth, and in the names of humanity and justice, will demand that something be done for the removal of slavery. Nay, without any such occasion, it must ere long appear, that the extreme doctrines and measures now urged in support of slavery, are not received unanimously, even at the south.

What then is in brief, the present state of the slavery question? It is just this. The anti-slavery societies, by their doctrine of immediate and unqualified abolition, and by the peculiar measures which they have adopted for the propagation of that doctrine, have divided the north and united the south. The southern agitators, by their doctrine of the superlative excellence and inviolable sacredness of slavery, and by their audacious demands in Congress and elsewhere, are rapidly making the north unanimous, and will ere long produce a division at the south. Then, when the voice of the north shall be again distinct, manly, true to its principles; and when some southern men shall again dare to maintain, that slavery is not the perfection of civilization —it will be found, that the cause of truth, of freedom, of happiness, while suffering temporary disaster, has been imperceptibly approaching the hour of final triumph.

Dr. Channing's book is well suited to do good just at this juncture. At the north, its eloquent appeals

will find a response in the mind of every man who
does not himself deserve to be a slave. The super-
ficial, sneering, infidel reply, which some anonymous author has published in Boston,* so far as it
has any effect on the public mind, must operate to
secure for the work before us a wider circulation, a
more attentive reading, and therefore a more decided
and salutary influence. At the south, its circulation
must of course be limited ; but there, hundreds of
leading men who would scorn to look upon a tract,
or a volume gratuitously circulated, are constrained
to buy it and to read it ; and however they may rage
against it or attempt to answer it, the time must
come, when the seed thus sown upon the angry
waters will have found a soil in which to vegetate.
The criticisms pronounced upon it by southern senators in Congress, will only go to promote that discussion of slavery which neither speeches, nor resolutions, nor laws, nor lawless violence, will be able
to suppress. Such speeches as that of the senator
from Virginia† are, if we may resume the figure we
have just been using, the wind which will help to
carry the scattered and floating seed to the spot
where, taking root, it will put forth first the blade,
then the ear, then the full corn in the ear.

At the hazard of seeming somewhat more discur-
sive than we are wont to be, we take leave to notice
one or two points in the speech of Mr. Leigh review-
ing Dr. Channing's book. The manliness and the

---

* Remarks on Dr. Channing's Slavery. By a citizen of Massachusetts. Boston, 1835.

† Mr. Leigh's speech on abolition of slavery in the District of Columbia. New-York Observer, Feb. 13, 1836.

gentlemanliness of that speech, entitle it to a degree of consideration which is not due to the vulgar and theatrical chivalry which many southern orators utter so profusely on such subjects. What then is the present state of the slavery question, as it appears in the honorable senator's critique on Dr. Channing?

First, if we do not altogether misunderstand the scope of Mr. Leigh's remarks, it is demanded, that the discussion of slavery and the publication of opinions concerning it shall be put down at the north, either by legislative enactments or by popular violence; and the question is, whether this demand shall be complied with. The senator's first and profoundest grief in regard to Dr. Channing's book is, that it is the Doctor's " purpose to counteract the efforts of those who are endeavoring to put down the schemes of the abolitionists, by embodying public opinion into efficient action against them." *Embodying public opinion into efficient action!* If any man is at a loss to decide what that means, let him look over a file of the New York Courier and Enquirer, or of the New York Evening Star, or of some of the agitating journals of those States in which the Lynch-court takes cognizance of all abuses of the freedom of speech.

Secondly, the doctrine is now laid down, that it is incendiary to declare that a man cannot *rightfully* be used as property. Dr. Channing uses this language: " We have thus seen, that a human being cannot rightfully be held and used as property. No legislation, not that of all countries or worlds could make him so. Let this be laid down as a first fundamental truth. Let us hold it fast, as a most sacred, precious truth. Let us hold it fast, against all customs, all laws, all rank, wealth, and power. Let it be armed with the whole authority of the civilized and Christian world." "Now," says the senator from Virginia in reply, "If Dr. Channing does not know, that such language as this is in its nature and tendency incendiary, I insist that he ought not to write upon any subject he so little understands." We say then, the question is, whether this doctrine shall be received as political and moral orthodoxy at the north. The question is not, whether the publisher of an incendiary book ought to be punished; it is, what makes the book incendiary?—it is, whether the author, the printer, and the publisher, who were concerned in getting up a paper or book which contains the opinion, that man, made in God's image, cannot *rightfully* be held and used as property, are incendiaries. Let every citizen of the free States make up his mind upon this question. FREE States, did we say? Nay, if this doctrine is to be admitted and established, Turkey is freer than New England.

Thirdly, it is a question between Dr. Channing and Mr. Leigh, whether slavery tends to licentiousness.

On this point, Dr. Channing has expressed himself eloquently and with great power. His language, which, in a single word, is perhaps a shade stronger than was necessary, need not be quoted here. Mr. Leigh says in reply, "I shall content myself with declaring my conscientious belief, that there is no society existing on the globe, in which the virtue of conjugal fidelity, in man as well as woman, and the happiness of domestic life, are more general than in

the slaveholding States." We cannot doubt that
Mr. Leigh believes as he says. Yet we cannot forget, that in those States the purity of a million of females is at the mercy of masters and of masters'
sons, living under a fervid clime, in idleness and
fullness of bread. We cannot forget, that among
more than two millions of people in those States
there is no such thing as legal marriage; that among
those two millions, the connections which they form
under the name of marriage, are always liable to be
dissolved, not only at the will of the parties, but
against their will, whenever the interest of a master or of a master's creditors may require a separation; and that, therefore, among two millions of
people there, the connection of husband and wife—
no, of male and female—can have nothing of the
sacredness that belongs to the relation of husband
and wife in a civilized and Christian community.
We cannot forget, that in those States females of
every variety of complexion, from the glossy ebony
to that slightest tinge of yellow through which the
quick blood speaks as eloquently, perhaps, as on the
cheek of the most delicate mistress, are liable to be
set up on a table in the most public places, exposed
like any other merchandise to the examination of
every idler passer by, and sold to the highest bidder;
and that the moment the purchaser has laid his hand
upon his bargain, she is as completely at his disposal
as if she had been sold in the slave-market of Tripoli,
to adorn the harem of a Turk. Some may find it
easy to believe, that every young master at the
south is a very Scipio; but we must forget what the
laws are in those States, and what human nature is

everywhere, before we can go as far as the senator from Virginia goes, in his vindication of the chastity of the southern slaves. The question, however, whether there is an actual connection between slavery and licentiousness, is a question more interesting and more important at the south than at the north. Let every southern man look around him and see what the facts are. Let every southern mother of a son ask herself, whether she believes that all mothers in the free States have just such anxieties as she has.

Dr. Channing touches on another part of this subject. He adverts to the fact, that many masters have children born into slavery. Most of these children, he presumes, are kindly treated during the life-time of the fathers; but, as the fathers die, not a few, especially since the obstacles in the way of emancipation have been increased, are left to the chances of slavery. " Still more, it is to be feared, that there are cases in which the master puts his own children under the whip of the overseer, or else sells them to undergo the miseries of bondage among strangers." " Among the pollutions of heathenism, I know nothing worse than this. The heathen who feasts on his country's foe, may hold up his head by the side of the Christian who sells his child for gain— sells him to be a slave. God forbid that I should charge this crime on a people. But however rarely it may occur, it is a fruit of slavery, an exercise of power belonging to slavery, and no laws restrain or punish it." To this the eloquent senator replies— how ?—by admitting all that Dr. Channing has said. " I shall not deny that such facts as he mentions

may have occurred. But," he proceeds, " is it reasonable, is it charitable, to allege such iniquities as
a reproach against our national character ?" Certainly, Mr. Senator, *so long as your laws tolerate and
uphold such villany*, so long your proud escutcheon
bears the stain in the face of all the world. When
your legislatures shall doom to the gallows or to the
penitentiary the man who sells his children, then
will that stain be wiped away. Mr Leigh proceeds
to say, that within a year he has seen several accounts of parents exposing their new-born infants in
the streets of the city of New York ; and he asks,
" Is there any man in his sound senses, that would
deduce from such facts matter of reproach against
the people of that city ?" We answer, perhaps not.
But why is it so ? Why are not the people there
responsible ? Simply because such exposures there
are held as crimes, not merely in the eye of conscience, but in the eye of law. The senator having
thrown up this little cloud of dust, makes good his
retreat from the point, by saying, " I believe that
the judicial records of this country will show that the
number of crimes, especially those of deepest atrocity,
committed in the non-slaveholding States, is much
greater than those committed in the slaveholding
States." Pray, Mr. Leigh, do the slaves in your
part of the country ever steal ? do they commit
adultery ? are they ever found guilty of assault and
battery upon each other ? and is there any " judicial
record" showing how often slaves are convicted of
such crimes ? Nay, if a slave should perpetrate a
rape upon the body of a slave, would there be any
" judicial record" of the crime ? If two gentlemen

have a brawl at a tavern, or a *rencontre* in the streets, and fight it out fairly and handsomely, with fists, with dirks, or with pistols, is there always some "judicial record" of the transaction? In general, does not the very existence of slavery, by making the master, in numberless instances, judge, jury, and executioner, and by keeping up among the lords of the soil a very peculiar sort of public sentiment, tend to diminish the number of "judicial records," rather than the number of crimes actually committed?

" Can the slaveholder use the word *amalgamation* without a blush?" To this question Mr. Leigh replies, " It is absolutely wonderful how little amalgamation has taken place in the course of two centuries." Wonderful it is to us, considering all the circumstances of the case; and yet we think, that if any man shall venture upon reading Dr. Channing's pungent question in the senate, when Col. Johnson shall have attained to the presidency of that body, there will be some expectation of a blush in certain quarters. But what is the great shame charged upon Col. Johnson by his political opponents at the south? Is it simply that he has a family of colored children? Or is it rather, that instead of treating his daughters as if they were cattle, he treats them with something of a father's affection, and even attempts to force them upon society, by taking them with him to places of public resort, and by marrying them to white men? We might name the governor of one of the proudest States of the Union, who permitted his daughter to be sold and transported from her native city to the painful and hopeless servitude of a plantation in Louisiana, when he might easily have saved her, and it was proposed to him to save her. Yet so little ignominy attaches to him on that account, that we presume not one in ten thousand of those who admire his greatness, can guess the name of the statesman and patriot who permitted his daughter to be sold into exile and slavery, when one word of his lips would have saved her. The African prince who should do the self-same thing on the banks of the Congo, would forfeit his character:

> ' But Brutus is an honorable man,
> So are they all, all honorable men.'

SLAVERY IN MARYLAND.*

[QUARTERLY CHRISTIAN SPECTATOR, 1836.]

THE author of this book was formerly, for several
years, Professor of Languages in the University of
North Carolina. Of course he has some qualifica-
tions for writing on slavery, which do not belong to
every man who undertakes to treat on that subject.
This book, however, contains the results, not so
much of his former acquaintance with slavery, as of
a tour performed by him last summer, with a view
to inquiries, in Maryland, Virginia and the District
of Columbia. It seems to have been written with
unusual candor. The author does not appear to
have commenced his inquiries with a predetermi-
nation as to the conclusions at which he should ar-
rive. We do not remember to have read anything
of the kind which seemed so entirely worthy of unqualified confidence.

The observations and inquiries which Mr. Andrews had the opportunity of making, in a tour of
three weeks, were necessarily limited; and any de-
ductions from them are, of course, liable to be modi-

---

* SLAVERY AND THE DOMESTIC SLAVE TRADE IN THE UNITED STATES.
In a series of letters addressed to the Executive Committee of the Ame-
rican Union for the relief and improvement of the colored race. By
Prof. E. A. ANDREWS. Boston, 1836.

fied by the results of more extended investigation. Yet there are some things in slavery, and in the condition of the colored population, which appear to a discerning observer at the first sight; and from which conclusions may be drawn which no subsequent investigation can set aside.

What is southern slavery in theory? This question can be answered, without going to the south at all. It can be accurately or fairly answered, only out of the statute-books of the States in which slavery exists. What is southern slavery in actual operation?—is quite another question. Putting our knowledge of the theory of slavery side by side with our knowledge of human nature, we may infer what this system will be in its actual operation. But this is only inference; and though no man who knows anything of human nature, can fail to acquire in this way some correct knowledge of the working of the system—every rational inquirer must feel that there may be—in the state of society, in the vital energy of the Christianity diffused, more or less extensively, through the community, in the power of public opinion uttered from all parts of the world; nay, even in the working of enlightened selfishness —counteracting and modifying influences not easily estimated. He must feel, too, that there may be, in the burning sun and enervating air of an almost Oriental climate, and in the excitement of commercial speculation, influences that even aggravate the natural operation of a system which, in theory, shocks all his sensibilities. The rational inquirer, then, cannot but presume, that the actual working of the system of slavery can only be completel and truly known by actual observation, or by the testimony of candid and faithful observers.

But what is the testimony of observers in respect to the operation of the system of slavery? One man, having traveled over the south, comes home with an account of the comforts of the slave, his contentment, the lightness of his tasks, his secure provision against the time of sickness or old age, his thoughtless merriment, and the contrast between his condition and that of the lazy, improvident, drunken, ungoverned and unprotected free black; and this is his picture of slavery. This, we need not say, is the very picture uniformly drawn by slaveholders. Another man will go over the same ground, and will see nothing but horrors, or at least will report nothing but horrors. The slave bleeding under the scourge, or fainting and dying under his burdens; the master indulging all the vices of the pirate; children torn from parents, and husbands from wives; these are the figures which fill up his representation. What shall we believe? Shall we receive all that is said by the one, and reject all that is said by the other? Certainly neither of these witnesses reports the whole truth; though probably each of them reports the whole impression produced on his mind by what he has seen. The observer who represents both sides of the subject, is the one whose story has in itself the strongest indications of complete trust-worthiness. There are slaves whose lot is simple wretchedness, without mixture, without alleviation, without hope. On the other hand, there are slaves well fed, well clothed, carefully protected and provided for, kindly and judiciously governed, whose yoke of

6

bondage is so light that it is hardly felt to be a yoke. To describe the lot of either of these classes ever so vividly, is not to give a full or fair account of slavery as it is in actual operation. The truth lies between these conflicting statements; or rather, the truth includes them both, and includes a great deal more. He whose interests or prejudices prevent him from seeing in slavery anything much to be regretted, and he whose feelings or predeterminations prevent him from reporting any alleviating circumstances, may both be valuable witnesses; for each may report facts of great importance, which the other entirely omits. Such a reporter, however, as the author of this book, is better than both of them. While he represents without fear or favor, and with natural sentiments of indignation, the atrocities which slavery produces, and which are the natural operation of the system, he has no passions and no perverted habits of mind, which prevent him from seeing or admitting into his statement the facts on which the slaveholder relies for the defence of the system. The following statement is one which seems to us important to a right apprehension of the subject :

'Among others into whose society I was accidentally thrown, were two families from the extreme south, who were returning slowly homeward from their summer's tour to the northern States, and stopping so long in the principal cities through which they passed, and at the various watering-places which they visited, as to reach Louisiana after the first frosts of autumn should have rendered their return safe. The gentlemen might have been twenty-five or thirty years old; the ladies were a few years younger. The latter had each the charge of an interesting child two or three years old, the special care of which was committed to two colored nurses, who were their only attendants. It was not easy to determine which of the group were happiest; the sedate, intelligent, and dignified fathers, the accomplished mothers, the playful children, or their young, well-fed, and well-dressed nurses.

The situation in which domestic slaves are often placed, in prosperous moral and intelligent families, is one of far more unmingled happiness than is usually imagined by those who have never witnessed it. The mistake into which many fall, upon this subject, arises principally from their failing to estimate properly the amount of happiness occasioned by the mutual affection between the white and the colored members of the same family. This attachment is of course a more available source of happiness in virtuous families, than in those of an opposite character; but, like parental and filial affection, it is rarely entirely wanting, even in the most hardened and profligate. This relation is in reality more like that of parent and child, than like any other with which it can be compared, and is altogether stronger than that which binds together the northern employer and his hired domestic. The slave looks to his master and mistress for direction in everything, and insensibly acquires for them a respect mingled with affection, of which those never dream who think of slavery only as a system of whips and fetters—of unfeeling tyranny, on the one part, and of fear mingled with hatred, on the other. The latter is the usual picture of slavery which is presented to the people of the north, and it is no wonder that southern masters, who know how wide from truth this representation is, are not particularly ready to listen to the counsel of those, whom they perceive to be so ill-informed upon the subject. Wanton cruelty may be too often practiced by masters, as it is by many parents; but this, which is but an occasional incident of slavery, should not be exhibited as the prominent evil. This may be removed by the influence of humane feelings, and especially by Christian principle; but countless evils will still remain, inherent and inseparable from the system.'—pp. 33-35.

Another aspect of slavery is exhibited in the following passage. It is in vain to tell a human being,

with a human heart, that slavery, however disguised,
is not " a bitter draught."

‘ It is sometimes said, that liberty is not greatly prized by the
slaves, or even by the free blacks themselves. I have seen the
attempt made to convince the slave that liberty would not place
him in more eligible circumstances. He would sometimes yield
to the arguments, but there was always something in his manner which showed that, even if the reason was confounded, the
heart did not yield its assent. Although the condition of the
free blacks in the southern States is proverbially wretched, and
most of them are sufficiently apprized of its inconveniences and
miseries by their own bitter experience, yet none of them manifest an inclination to return to slavery. Fully acquainted with
both conditions, they submit to the inconveniences of freedom,
not indeed contentedly, but with no design of improving their
circumstances by sacrificing their liberty. While residing at the
south, I knew an intelligent free mulatto, whose name was Sam.
I do not remember in what manner he obtained his freedom, but
he richly deserved it by his uniformly good behavior. A friend
of mine who took a deep interest in his welfare, often conversed
kindly with him concerning his prospects, and endeavored to
suggest plans for his benefit. He was struck with the unfortunate circumstances in which the free blacks were placed, and
once endeavored to convince Sam that his condition had not been
improved by obtaining his liberty. Sam listened to his repre-
sentations in respectful silence, conscious of his own inability to
maintain the cause of freedom by an array of argument. When
my friend had concluded his appeal, Sam's only answer was,
" AFTER ALL, IT'S A HEAP BETTER TO BE FREE." Brief, however,
as the answer was, it spoke the feelings of the whole human
race, whether bond or free. If liberty could ever be accounted
worthless, it would be such a liberty as falls to the lot of the
free negro, when surrounded by slaves and their masters. Yet,
with no better prospects than these, he was able to decide, with
a clearness of apprehension that nothing could confuse or mislead,
that freedom was still invaluable. While this principle remains
in full operation in the heart, it is in vain that the slave is convinced that his external circumstances would not be improved by

obtaining his freedom : though satisfied that by remaining a slave
he shall be better fed, and clothed, and sheltered, and nursed
when sick or old, he still feels that the power to choose for himself and to direct his own actions, is more than an equivalent for
all these advantages, and his heart replies, " *After all, it's a heap
better to be free.*" '—pp. 107–109.

What is slavery in the city of Washington ?—the
slavery which is too sacred to be touched by the exclusive jurisdiction of Congress? The facts described below occurred last summer. Our author's
informant was " a gentleman well known in this
country for his literary and scientific attainments."

' A negro, about twenty-five years old, who is married, and
has three or four children, has just applied to my informant,
stating that he is to be sold immediately to a slave-dealer, and
separated forever from his family, unless he can find some resi-
dent in the District who will consent to purchase him. He is a
member of a church in this city, and has uniformly sustained a
Christian character. His master wishes to raise a few hundred
dollars, which he has not the means of doing conveniently, without the sale of one of his slaves. Now it happens that the purpose for which this money is to be raised is well known, and
is no other than to purchase a mulatto woman, with whom he is
known to be criminally connected. As if even this were not a
sufficient provocation to the moral sense of the community, there
is an aggravation arising from the motive which determined the
master to sell the slave of whom I am speaking, rather than any
other. He had endeavored to employ this slave in bringing other
colored women into the same relation to him, as the mulatto
woman whom I have mentioned, but here the servant felt that
he had a Master in heaven, whom he was bound to obey, rather
than his earthly master. His refusal had greatly irritated his
master, and led to his being selected for sale.'—pp. 111, 112.

*   *   *   *   *   *   *   *

One of the most interesting topics in the whole
field of inquiry respecting slavery and abolition, is
the progress of Maryland toward becoming a free

State.   Some facts in relation to this subject have
been collected by Mr. Andrews, which are well
worthy to be considered by all who would understand what prospect there is of the abolition of slavery.   It is only to be regretted that these facts, instead of being scattered here and there through a
series of somewhat familiar letters, were not arranged
and combined in such forms as to show more distinctly the great principles which they involve.
Perhaps, however, the book might in that way
have lost in popular interest more than it would
have gained in philosophical precision.

"In this State," says our author, "*slave-labor employed in agriculture has long since ceased, with few
exceptions, to be valuable.*" This everybody knows
already; and everybody knows the reason of it.
Slave-labor, in Maryland, comes into competition
with free-labor, and is therefore unprofitable.   And
when the political economists of the south have
"exhausted the argument" for the superior profitableness of slave-labor in agriculture, it is answer
enough to point to the agriculture of Maryland, and
to demand of them an instance in which free labor
has become unprofitable when placed in competition,
on equal terms, with the labor of slaves.   Slave-
labor then must cease to be profitable everywhere,
just in proportion as the labor of freemen can be
employed in the production of the same commodities.
Let the time come when the labor of intelligent
freemen shall produce cotton, rice, and sugar, on a
large scale, and slave-labor will cease to be more
profitable in the agriculture of Louisiana and Mississippi, than it is in the agriculture of Maryland.

In consequence of the unprofitableness of slave-labor, *there is an increasing desire among the citizens of Maryland to be rid of slavery.* The transportation of slaves by thousands to the southern States, does not indeed indicate such a desire. But other things mentioned by our author, do indicate the desire in Maryland to become a free State. No serious legal difficulties are thrown in the way of emancipation. The testimony of one respectable witness, that he is well acquainted with the party, and that he knows him to bear a fair character for honesty and temperance, is regarded by the courts as sufficient to secure for the emancipated slave the privilege of a continued residence within the State. Emancipations are frequent, and are increasingly popular. It is stated that not fewer than fifteen hundred slaves had been manumitted within the three and a half years preceding the date of our author's inquiries; and that the majority of these were manumitted without reference to their emigration. Can it be doubted, that if at any time slave-labor should become equally unprofitable in the more southern States, there will be in those more southern States the same disposition to be rid of slavery which now exists in Maryland?

Slavery in Maryland is actually on the wane. The number of slaves has been, for a quarter of a century, continually diminishing. At the first census, viz., in 1790, the number was 103,036. At the end of ten years the increase had been 2.52 per cent. During another ten years the increase was 5.55 per cent.; so that in 1810 the number of slaves was 111, 502, or 8,466 more than in 1790. From 1810 to 1820, the *decrease* was 3.68 per cent.; and from

1820 to 1830, it was 4.1 per cent.; so that in 1830 the slave population of that State was less than it was in 1810 by 8,508. The white population in the meanwhile has increased in a constantly increasing ratio—for the first ten years, 3.68 per cent.; for the second, 8.68; for the third, 10.67; for the fourth, 11.87. The time is not far distant, then, when Maryland will be numbered with the free States. Must not other States in their turn yield to the same influences, and become free?

The diminution of the slave population in Maryland, has been accompanied with a great increase of the free colored population. In 1790 the number of free colored persons in Maryland was only 8,043. In 1830 the number was 52,938, making an increase of 558 per cent. in forty years. From 1820 to 1830, the increase was 33.24 per cent., just about three times as great as the increase of the white population for the same period. It is to be noticed, however, that since the prohibition of the foreign slave-trade, the increase of the entire colored population, bond and free, has not been rapid. In the ten years, from 1800 to 1810, the increase was 16.13 per cent. But from 1810 to 1820, it was only 1.17 per cent. From 1820 to 1830, it was 5.98 per cent. If Maryland has her Prof. Dew, let him tell us how much the internal slave-trade has to do with this diminished per centage. But however this may be, the great increase of the *free* colored population, is proof decisive of the tendency toward emancipation.

Some indications of the same kind appear in other States. In Virginia, the increase of the free blacks in the ten years preceding the last census, was

27.49 per cent. ; that of the slaves, for the same period, was only 11.85 per cent. ; that of the whites, 15.12 per cent. In North Carolina, for the same period, the increase of the free blacks was 33.74 per cent. ; that of the slaves, 19.79 per cent. ; that of the whites 12.79 per cent. In Kentucky, the increase of the free colored population, for the same period, was 67.18 per cent. ; that of the slaves, 30.36 per cent.; that of the whites, 19.12 per cent. In Tennessee, the increase of the free blacks for the same period, was 63.9 per cent. In Ohio, which, bordering upon a slave region, receives a great share of the slaves emancipated in the neighboring States, the increase of free blacks for the same period, was 96.91 per cent. In Indiana, during the same period, 2,499 free blacks were added to their numbers, making the increase of this portion of their population 195.04 per cent. These statistics show, that emancipation is all the while going on, not in Maryland alone, but in all the States in which the profits of slave labor are diminishing. Taking the whole Union together, no class of population increases so rapidly as the free blacks.

But what will be the result of emancipation in the more northern slave States ? Will the emancipated population be removed ? Will they be employed as laborers upon the soil ? Will they coalesce with the white population, sharing with them on equal terms in all the employments of society ? These are questions not to be answered with much certainty ; yet some of the statements made by our author may be regarded as affording materials for an approximation to a correct answer.

6*

In Maryland, *the labor of the free blacks is not considered valuable.* There, as at the north, they are found, not in the country laboring upon the soil, not in the workshop or manufactory, where work is to be done with steady application, but congregated in the cities. In Baltimore alone, which contains not one twenty-fifth part of the slaves of Maryland, nearly two-fifths of the free blacks maintain their existence, living by just such employments as support the free blacks in New York and the cities of New England.

The labor of white men is superseding the labor both of slaves and of the free people of color. In those employments which require severe and steady effort, not only is a decided preference given to the labor of white men, but white laborers are found in sufficient numbers to meet the demand. Mr. Andrews tells us, that all the great public works in Maryland have been constructed almost exclusively by the hands of Irishmen. He tells us furthermore, what every traveler passing that way has occasion to observe, that even in Baltimore, the Irish and other foreigners are competitors with the blacks for employment as porters, carmen, ostlers, and domestic sevants. There is a constant immigration of foreign laborers into Baltimore. We find among our memoranda the following fact, stated at the time in one of the newspapers of that city. Between the first and the twenty-fifth of June, 1833, nearly seventeen hundred emigrants from Europe, of whom about one hundred and fifty were Irish, and the remainder nearly all Germans and Swiss, arrived at Baltimore, and were expected to settle in that part of the coun-

try. Such facts show, that in that region the labor
of white men is likely to supersede the labor of the
free blacks, as well as of the slaves. A similar competition exists to some extent in almost every part
of the country. An intelligent gentleman from
South Carolina, who had no theory to support, remarked to Mr. Andrews, that even there, Irishmen
were ready to do anything that the free blacks might
be wanted to do.

Yet it is not impossible for the free blacks to
find employment. The demand for labor is so great
in this country, that all sorts of laborers are in request. In New York it is remarked, that the colored
people, by their address and ingenuity, contrive to
monopolize, to a considerable extent, a certain class
of employments, and to turn over to their Irish competitors the more toilsome business of carrying mortar, breaking stone, or digging and plying the wheel-
barrow upon roads and canals. In Baltimore, Mr.
A. observed, that many of the free people of color
were much better dressed than the lower class of
white people, particularly the Irish. As domestic
servants, those colored people who have been brought
up to that business are far better than any others in
this country. Thousands of the better sort of the
free colored people at the south, might find immediate employment in New England, to the great relief
of many a householder, whose daily grief is to hear
the groanings of his helpmate over the unskillfulness
and misrule of her kitchen cabinet, and the difficulty, so unheard of in politics, of filling vacant places.

*The mortality among the blacks is greater than in
any other class of the community.* For eleven years,

the record of deaths in the city of Baltimore has carefully distinguished the three classes of white, free blacks, and slaves. The deaths among the free blacks annually, are one in twenty-nine; among the whites, one in thirty-eight; among the slaves, only one in forty-four. If distinct records of the deaths in each of these three classes were kept everywhere, the proportion might not indeed be everywhere the same; but there is great reason to believe, that similar results would everywhere appear. Mr. Andrews suggests the inquiry, whether it may not be that slavery alone prevents the colored race in the United States from a gradual extinction. Let us see what facts there are to answer this inquiry. The colored population of Massachusetts increased at the rate of only 2.62 per cent. in the ten years preceding the last census. Yet Massachusetts, while she sends out no colored emigrants, is every summer receiving into her metropolis colored emigrants from other States. Rhode Island has large towns to give refuge and employment to the colored people; yet in Rhode Island, for twenty years before the last census, the colored population was slowly decreasing. Connecticut sends no colored people to Georgia, to Illinois, or to Liberia; but, on the contrary, her cities are continually receiving colored people from the south; yet in Connecticut the increase of the colored population, for the ten years preceding the last census, was only 0.38 per cent. None of our readers need to be reminded how the colored people from all the south crowd into the great cities of New York; yet the increase of the colored population of that State was only 12.17 per cent. in ten years. In

New Jersey the increase was less than two per cent.
Now cut off from these northern States the supply
that pours from the south, and how long would
there be here any colored population to be counted?

We have no room to go into the theory of this
subject. Let it suffice to indicate one or two principles. The only possible check upon the growth of
a slave population must be either the cruelty of the
master, or his absolute inability to give them food.
No moral "preventive check," no prudence, no
dread of poverty, can prevent slaves from fulfilling
to the utmost that great mandate, "increase and
multiply." And when the children are once
brought into the world, they are not the children of
paupers, exposed to the wants, the perils, the dis-
eases of poverty; they belong to a rich man, who
must feed them and provide for them, if he be not a
monster. But when the slaves become free, all the
checks upon population begin to operate. And the
more sudden the emancipation, the more rapid will
be the working of these checks.

What, then, may we anticipate, as the destiny of
the colored population of this country? If there are
districts of this country, where the climate forbids
the white man to labor, those districts will undoubtedly be inhabited by blacks. But in every other
part, will not the white man be ultimately the laborer and the sole possessor? It is not for us to answer this question positively. We only say, that the
question is worth studying.

LETTER

TO THE EDITOR OF THE PHIL. CHRISTIAN OBSERVER, 1845.

———

[As the following letter is referred to on a subsequent page, and as it contains not only an outline of the following series, but some thoughts which are not repeated elsewhere, it seems proper to give it a place in this collection. It explains for itself the occasion on which it was written.]

———

MR. EDITOR:—Some person has been kind enough to send me your paper of the 5th instant, in which a writer, subscribing himself "A Puritan at the South," animadverts with some freedom upon a speech which he supposes me to have made at the last meeting of the General Association of Connecticut, and of which he has found some representation in the Boston Recorder. I have not seen the Boston Recorder to which he refers, and therefore I cannot say whether the report of my speech there is correct or not. I only know that elsewhere I have seen it decidedly mis-reported.

The passage which your correspondent has quoted from my speech, is not a very unfair representation of something which I said, if the connection in which it was said is fairly given by the reporter—which I am bound to presume is not the case, inasmuch as your correspondent makes no allusion to the course of my argument, on which the meaning of that passage entirely depends. I said nothing in that speech, I believe, which I have not often said in print, with at least equal strength of language, years ago; and because I have taken just the position which I took in that speech, those who in this part of the country call themselves the only "friends of the slave," have made me—as your correspondent knows, if he knows anything about me in this relation—a mark of special obloquy.

My positions were, in effect, and "for substance," briefly these:

1. The *relation* of master to one whom the laws and the constitution of society have made a slave, is not intrinsically and necessarily a sin on the part of the master; certainly not such a sin as will justify a sentence of excommunication against him, without inquiry as to how he came into that relation, or how he conducts himself in it.

2. The master who buys and sells human beings, like cattle, for gain; who permits male and female servants, placed by law under his protection and control, to live together in brutish concubinage, or in a merely temporary pairing, with no religious sanctity, which is not only unprotected by the law, but which he himself considers liable to be dissolved at the caprice of the parties, or whenever his convenience or gain may require the separation; who refuses to train his servants diligently, from their childhood up, in the knowledge of God and in the way of salvation, and of the book of God, and whose servants, in a word, live and die in heathenish igno-

rance ; or who treats his servants in any manner inconsistent with the fact that they are intelligent and voluntary beings who were created in God's image, and for whom Christ has died—does not make a creditable profession of Christian piety. Such a master has no more claim to recognition or communion among Christ's disciples than a Turk might have, who, having renounced Mohammed, might present himself for membership in a Christian church while yet retaining a full "patriarchal" seraglio of wives and concubines.

3. It is not to be presumed that all masters, professing to be "believing masters," are, of course, guilty of all or any of the crimes above described. But so far as the ministers, elders, or members of any church commit any of these crimes, and the church to which they are responsible in respect to their Christian character, does not deal with them as offenders, to bring them to repentance, or if they will not repent, to cut them off as reprobate, so far that church is liable to be called to account by every and any church with which it is in communion. And it is the duty of all churches with which a church so neglecting the discipline of Christ's house may desire communion, to admonish that church, and labor with it for its reformation, and, in the event of the failure of such efforts, then to withdraw from all communion with it.

4. Those laws of the southern States, by the force of which the crimes above mentioned, and others of the same general description, instead of being forbidden and punished, are permitted and promoted, are a shame to human nature, especially when con-

sidered as the laws of a people glorying in their freedom, their honor, and (*proh pudor*) their magnanimity. The *system* of slavery in these United States, as it exists in its own theory, apart from any question of fact in respect to the working of the system—the system of slavery, simply as set forth in the laws respecting slavery—is a system which belongs, historically and philosophically, to the lowest stage, save one, of human barbarism. The existence of such a body of laws in the statute-books of free American states, " Anglo Saxon " in lineage, and pretending to be Christian, is enough to make the cheek of an American, anywhere, tingle with shame. It is often said that no people can be, on the whole, better than their laws are. I believe that thousands of the southern people are a great deal better than their laws are. I try all I can to believe that the entire people of the south are better, in fact, than they are, as represented by their laws—though sometimes, I must confess, I have to try very hard, especially when such events happen as that which happened a few days ago at Lexington, and that which happened last winter at Charleston. I do believe that there are thousands of southern men whose moral sense is shocked, as mine is, by the atrocity of those defences of slavery which are put forth now and then by the Hammonds, the McDuffies, and the Dews. But, after all, the fact remains. Those barbarian laws stand in the statute-books; and of the thousands who at heart detest them, *who* dares to propose a repeal or an amendment? Who dares even to utter a protest against them? Public opinion at the south—or what passes for public opinion—

annihilates, on this subject, the freedom of the press, the freedom of speech, and even the right of private judgment. No people upon earth are more governed by public opinion, or have less idea of the possibility of resisting public opinion, than the people of our southern States, particularly in relation to this subject. Public opinion makes them murder each other —like cowards who dare not refuse to do what they know to be wrong—in duels. Public opinion, speaking in the hoarse clamors of the blood-thirsty mob, and in the terrific sentence of the Lynch court, compels the thousands who detest those laws about slavery to digest their detestation in silence. This very habit of being governed by a local public opinion, and of regarding public opinion as a force that cannot possibly be resisted, makes the southern people, in proportion as their intercourse with other communities increases, and the eyes of the nations are turned with closer attention towards their " peculiar institutions," more and more sensitive to the public opinion of the world at large. "They that take the sword, shall perish by the sword." So they who attempt to uphold an atrocious body of laws by the tyranny of public opinion, are already beginning to writhe under the indignant public opinion of the civilized world. I say, then, let the voice of universal human nature utter itself against those laws.

It is not through any want of sensibility to shame, but only through ignorance and thoughtlessness of what the public opinion of the world really is, that citizens of the States in which that atrocious system of laws exists, are able to look citizens of other States, or the subjects of other governments, in the face without blushing. What Virginian or Carolinian would not blush, to be told at a northern watering-place, in the presence of enlightened foreigners—Sir, the laws of your State permit a man to sell his own son, as he would a mule; or his own daughter, only a shade yellower than himself, as he would sell a horse. What stuff is that chivalry made of, that would not cower to be told that in the chivalrous land of the sunny south, the chastity of more than a million of women is without a shadow of legal protection—that the father, the brother, or the husband of one of those women, if he should lift his hand against the seducer or the ravisher, might be killed on the spot, as if he were a mad dog? I cannot believe that the people of the south—the more intelligent portion of them particularly—are so insensible to the public opinion of the world as not to care what the world thinks of these laws of theirs, which, instead of requiring the master to render to his servants that which is just and equal, forbid his paying them wages; which, instead of requiring the master to see that his servants receive such an education as an enlightened State ought to furnish for every human being reared under its jurisdiction, make it a crime to teach a slave the alphabet; and which, instead of regarding the slave as a being having personal rights, even against his master, make it impossible for the master to endow him with any rights whatever.

Your correspondent, Mr. Editor, and what is of more consequence, your readers, can see whether my language is, as he affirms, " sufficiently indiscriminate and abusive to gratify the feelings of the

most thorough-going political revilers of the day."
In my views, and in my language, I ' discriminate'
carefully between the *relation* of a master to one
whom society has made a slave, and the *conduct* of
that master in that relation—or in other words, between the *power* of doing wrong which the law
gives to the master as against the slave, and the *use*
which the master makes of that power.   I ' discriminate' carefully between the *churches* of the south
and the offences of *individuals* in communion with
those churches, and instead of excommunicating all
*slaveholders simply as such, and all churches which
contain slaveholders*, I would, in the discharge of a
fraternal duty, call upon the southern churches
themselves to put in force the discipline of Christ's
house against *specific sins*, which their own moral
sense acknowledges to be incompatible with the
credibility of a Christian profession.   I also ' discriminate' between the *laws* of the Southern States
respecting slavery and the blacks, and the individual *citizens* of those States ; and while I regard those
laws with unlimited abhorrence as a disgrace to my
country and a disgrace to the human species, I regard the people of those States as better than their
laws—thousands of them a great deal better.   I am
willing to treat individual citizens of slaveholding
States with all the courtesy and respect due to gentlemen and to American fellow-citizens, except as I
find individuals unworthy of such treatment.   But
they on the other hand must allow me, here at home,
a freeman's privilege of abhorring slavery and of
uttering my abhorrence.   So I could treat a gentle-
manly Turk or Persian with courtesy and hospitali-

ty in my New England home, but he must not require me to give up my Christian and American opinions, out of complaisance to his Islamism and his polygamy.

Your correspondent seems to intimate that I, as living in a free-labor State, am necessarily too ignorant on the subject of slavery to have any opinion worth regarding. As if a man could not tell whether it is wrong to buy and sell human beings at public auction " in lots to suit purchasers," without living in a slave State. As if the public opinion of a slave State, armed with the furies of Lynch law, and assuming an unlimited arbitrary power over every man's private judgment (unless it is very private indeed) were a necessary guide for erring human nature to a knowledge of the right and wrong about slavery. As if I, living here, where every man is free to think and free to speak on every side, and where I have had the privilege of receiving through the post-office no fewer than three copies of Gov. Hammond's defence of slavery, were less competent to form an unbiased opinion, than I should be if I lived where no man is allowed to speak but on one side, and where, if I should be so unfortunate as to form an opinion contrary to public opinion, and should be found out in it, the least that I, as a northern man, could expect, would be to be arrayed in tar and feathers, unless I should make my escape as a felon flees from justice.

Your correspondent farther suggests that if I " would reform the institutions of the south," I ought to " come and dwell" there, where the work is to be done. Let me say then, that I have not undertaken to reform the institutions of the south. I leave that work in the hands of the people of the south to whom it belongs, and whom God will hold accountable for it. I acknowledge the kindness of your correspondent's hospitable invitation, but God has given me a better lot. " The lines are fallen to me in pleasant places." I find myself where all the work that I can do comes daily to my hands; and I do not conceive that, considering all my relations, I could do more for the kingdom of Christ, or the welfare of my country there, than I can here. If God had cast my lot there, I would stay there; for nowhere upon earth can more good be done by a good man who is native on the soil and has the confidence of the people, than there. I would not go on a foreign mission, and leave that field behind me; it were as wise to go from China on a foreign mission to Kamschatka. Least of all would I, like some southern ministers, seek a settlement at the north for the sake of getting away from slavery.

Respectfully yours,

LEONARD BACON.

New-Haven, Sept. 8, 1845.

THE COLLISION

BETWEEN THE

ANTI-SLAVERY SOCIETY AND THE AMERICAN BOARD.

———

[NEW YORK EVANGELIST, 1846.]

———

To the Editors of the New-York Evangelist:

GENTLEMEN:—I have felt myself called to prepare the following papers, because I see, in some quarters, evidence that the question between the Anti-Slavery Society and the Foreign Missionary Board needs once more to be distinctly stated, and that the position of the Board is not fairly understood. I send the papers to you, asking a place for them in the columns of your journal, instead of attemptirg any other form of publication, because 1 know not in what other way I can reach so many of those readers who are in a state of mind to be influenced by the views which I wish to present.

The extent to which my name has been used in connection with this subject, seems on the whole to require that what I publish shall be on my own responsibility.   Yours, &c.,

LEONARD BACON.

New-Haven, Jan. 22, 1846.

NO. I.—THE QUESTION STATED.

AMONG the many mischievous effects of slavery in its unnatural connection with our republican and Christian institutions, is that erratic philanthropy which has usurped the name of abolitionism. There is so much in slavery that excites the mind to indignation; the subject, at the same time, is so compli-

cated in its nature and relations, touching upon so
many interests, commercial, political, and religious;
that there is no wonder we find opposition to slavery
continually tending to extravagances of statement
and of action. So it will be while slavery continues. The odious and atrocious injustice of the system is enough to " make a wise man mad ;" how
much more will it inflame to madness those whose
feelings are more than a match for their wisdom.

The Anti-Slavery Societies of the northern States,
as is well known, have been for many years coming
into frequent collision with all sorts of religious and
philanthropic bodies. This has come to pass on the
part of the anti-slavery leaders, not in mere malice
or for the sake of working mischief, but in the belief
that if the religious and philanthropic bodies in this
part of the country can all be made auxiliary to the
Anti-Slavery Society, then that Society will be strong
enough to abolish slavery. Under the influence of
such a belief, colleges, theological seminaries,
churches and ecclesiastical organizations, Tract, Bible, and Missionary Societies, have all been assailed,
with various success.

The American Board of Commissioners for Foreign Missions, has been to these reformers an object
of special regard. So extensive have been the operations of that institution ; so signal has been the success of some of its missions; and so great is the confidence with which it is honored by the New England churches, and by churches elsewhere, of New
England sympathies ; that it has seemed to anti-
slavery leaders to be just the instrument with which
to accomplish their great design. If the Board of

Foreign Missions could only be brought into an auxiliary relation to the Anti-Slavery Society, then surely the anti-slavery cause would triumph.

Accordingly from year to year, for I know not how long, the anti-slavery question in one form or another has been brought, by memorial or otherwise, into the conventions of the Board. To go into the history of these proceedings would perhaps be tedious. A summary may be found in a pamphlet lately published by the Prudential Committee, which is probably within the reach of as many as would take any special interest in reading it. I will say, however, that in my opinion the principal error in the proceedings of the Board heretofore—if there has been error on their part—has been, that they have not given, in answer to the various applications that have been made to them from time to time, a brief and peremptory definition of their principles in the form of distinct and well-considered propositions, such as might be easily taken into the mind and easily remembered. The action of the Board has not been in the form of resolutions affirming or denying certain propositions respecting slavery ; but only in the form of the acceptance of an essay, or a diplomatic reply to the memorialists, from a committee. In connection with this, there has *seemed* to be some sort of reluctance to meet the question face to face. Much has been said, and to very little purpose in my view, about the " one object" of the Board, the propagation of the gospel, and about the impropriety of turning aside from that great and good work for the sake of settling questions about slavery, or for the sake of co-operating in particular

7

schemes of reformation; whereas, nothing is more palpable than that if the Anti-Slavery Society, as represented by its publications and its executive officers, is right—if the master of a slave, simply as such, without any reference to his treatment of the slave, is " a man-stealer," and is to be considered by all Christians as a heathen man and a publican—then it is the duty of the Board, as a society instituted for the one purpose of propagating the gospel, to say so outright without regard to consequences, and to instruct its Prudential Committee and all its agents and missionaries, to adopt that principle unswervingly in all its applications.   And on the other hand, if the one only characteristic principle of the Anti-Slavery Society is, as I do earnestly believe, a miserable, paltering, juggling sophism, that can have no better effect than to mislead and madden enthusiastic minds, and to irritate the passions of the slaveholder while it sears his conscience—then, at the very first obtrusion of this principle, it ought to have been met with a firm and peremptory denial, in language not to be misunderstood.   But the successive reports which have been presented by committees and accepted by the Board, have so carefully abstained from the abstract assertion of general principles, have had so much to do with the statement and explanation of particular facts, and have shown so much desire to conciliate the anti-slavery movement, that the leaders of that movement have been encouraged with the hope of ultimate success. It was quite natural for them to reason that if agitation had accomplished so much, then more agitation ould accomplish more.

The late annual meeting of the Board, at Brooklyn, was signalized by a discussion of slavery in its relations to the missionary work. Never before had the subject been debated in that body. Many feared the occurrence of such a discussion as a great evil. Many apprehended that it would be accompanied with popular excitement, and with such scenes of agitation as have accompanied similar discussions in other religious and philanthropic assemblies. At former meetings, the subject had been considered only in committees—the reports of the committees being presented near the close of the session, and adopted without debate. But in this instance, the discussion was anticipated by those who planned the arrangement of business for the meeting; and everything was very properly allowed to give way before the paramount urgency of the anti-slavery question. The debate occupied the greater part of the entire session. It was *free ;* there was no restraint put upon the utterance of any opinion, however extreme. On the one hand, there were the strongest denunciations, not only of slavery, but of all who are masters of slaves—on the other hand there was a speech from a South Carolina clergyman, suited exactly to the meridian of Charleston— and both were heard with exemplary patience. The discussion was bold, partly in consequence of its being free ; every man who spoke seemed to express his opinion without fear of giving offence. At the same time, it was characterized by *decorum.* Though the number of members present, corporate and honorary, was more than six hundred, all of whom had the same right to speak ; and though, in

the absence of all concert or consultation as to who
should lead in the argument, some fifty or more were
ready and anxious to take part in the debate ; there
was no unseemly contending for the floor, and only
once or twice was there any occasion for a call to order.
And notwithstanding the necessarily desultory character of an unprepared debate, on such a subject, in
such an assembly, all will agree that it was on the
whole an uncommonly *able* discussion. On the
part of the Anti-Slavery Society, the leader in the
debate was the Rev. Amos A. Phelps, the Society's
principal secretary ; a man not surpassed in logical
acumen, or in the capacity of seeing the force of distinctions and arguments, or in controversial experience, by any of the chiefs of that organization; a
man who having given the best years of his life,
and the powers of a well-cultivated mind, to the
study and practice of anti-slavery as a profession,
and having made himself familiar with all depart-
ments of the subject, needed not, like some others,
to retail the stereotyped common-places of fourth-rate
anti-slavery lectures. On the other side, it will not
be invidious to mention the speeches of Dr. Edward
Beecher and Prof. Stowe, as characterized by eminent learning and great force of argument.

The form in which the question presented itself
for discussion on that occasion, was perhaps the
very best form in which it could arise. In other
forms in which the question might have been presented, it would have been entangled with side
questions of expediency ; so that many individuals,
dissenting entirely from the characteristic principle
of the Anti-Slavery Society, might have been con-

strained to vote with the adherents of that principle. Thus, had the question been on the employment of slave-owners as missionaries, the men who hold the doctrine of the Anti-Slavery Society would have answered in the negative, because the slave-owner, as they judge, is in every possible case a man-stealer; and at the same time many others would have answered in the negative with equal emphasis, for very different reasons—such as that the slave-owner owes to the slaves who in the providence of God are under his protection, certain duties which require him to remain with them—and that if he is the right man in other respects for the foreign missionary work, he is more likely to do good in South Carolina or Mississippi than in Syria or Africa. Or had the question been whether to send agents to the southern churches, soliciting their contributions, the consistent upholders of the Anti-Slavery Society would have answered, No, because the southern churches admit slaveholders to communion, and because, in their judgment, every such church is no better than a synagogue of Satan; while many others would also have said, No, as thinking that the contributions thus realized would not repay the expense and trouble accruing—or as of opinion that the southern churches have more missionary work among the black heathen within their own borders, than they are likely to attend to—or as judging that any attempt at extensive co-operation between the northern churches and the southern, is likely to result in painful collisions, and to hinder instead of promoting the natural action of Christianity against slavery. But in this instance the only question that could legitimately be raised, was the question whether every slave-master is to be excommunicated from the church, simply as standing in that relation.

Perhaps I may be allowed briefly to recall the leading facts of the case to the remembrance of my readers. Negro slavery, it seems, has existed for more than sixty years, to a limited extent, in the Cherokee and Choctaw nations of Indians. The churches formed by the missionaries in those two nations, have received to communion some few individuals who are the owners of slaves. This fact having been seized upon by the Anti-Slavery Society, memorials were sent to the Board, from some very respectable sources, requesting that the Board would take " such action as shall speedily remove the evil." At the meeting in 1844, these memorials were put into the hands of a committee, consisting of Rev. Dr. Woods and Rev. David Sandford and David Greene, of Masssachusetts; Rev. Dr. Tyler and Hon. T. W. Williams, of Connecticut; Chancellor Walworth and Rev. J. W. McLane, of New York; Rev. Dr. Tappan and Rev. S. L. Pomeroy, of Maine, and Rev. Dr. Stowe, of Ohio. Of these gentlemen, two, Dr. Woods, and Mr. Greene, are probably the only individuals against whom the Anti-Slavery Society had any special prejudice; three, Dr. Tappan, Mr. Sandford and Mr. Pomeroy, call themselves, and are commonly called, abolitionists, and are, it is believed, members of the Anti-Slavery Society; Mr. Sandford was himself one of the memorialists. It was the duty of this Committee to obtain information respecting the facts alleged and complained of by the memorialists, and to report at the meeting in 1845. Nor did the gentlemen perform their duty negligently. Every one of them, except Mr. Pomeroy, who was absent in Europe, attended to the business in person. After the necessary information had been obtained by correspondence with the missions, the Committee met to agree on their report. The draft of a report, which had been prepared by the chairman, was not entirely satisfactory ; and after a full discussion of the principles that were to be asserted and adhered to, it was put into the hands of a sub-committee. At a later meeting, the sub-committee presented a new draft, which, after further discussion and amendment, was agreed to as the report of the Committee, and in that form was presented to the Board at Brooklyn.

The form of the report—the ordinary form of reports in that body—had this disadvantage, that in the discussion and decision there was a necessity of taking, or rejecting it, as a whole. There was no series of propositions to be separately discussed, and separately voted on. Some of the most important principles of the case are introduced indirectly, and as it were, by the way, rather than put forward with as much prominence as some might desire. All that the report contains, and all that it does not contain, could hardly be ascertained by the mere hearer, at one reading, or even at two. The representatives of the Anti-Slavery Society, however, were not long in perceiving that it did not contain their doctrine directly or indirectly. It was not enough for them to see, that it condemns the institution of slavery as an institution at war with natural justice and with all the principles and designs of the gospel, and as an arrangement which the legitimate influence of the gospel will surely abolish ; it must go farther, if it is to please them.   All the injustice and mischievousness of the institution, it must impute to every individual whom that institution invests with power over his fellow-men ; and it must pronounce anathema against him, without inquiring how he administers that power.   Accordingly Mr. Phelps, at an early stage of the debate, proposed an amendment in two parts, for the purpose of making the report agree precisely with the peculiar and characteristic dogma of his Society.   He moved to amend the report as follows :

1. By inserting the words, " and practice," after the words " system," in all those passages which speak of the system as wicked, unrighteous, &c., so that they will read " the wickedness of the system and practice of slavery." &c., &c.

2. By appending the following as the conclusion of the report, viz.:

" In conclusion, the Board adopt the following preamble and resolutions as a summary exposition of the views and principles embodied in the foregoing remarks, and of the rules that should govern the Executive officers and missionaries of the Board in their practical application.

Whereas, in the providence of God, this Board, in conducting its operations among the Indians and elsewhere, has been brought into such contact with slavery as to demand some judgment of the Board respecting its moral character, and the adoption of some general rules of conduct for the guidance of its Executive officers and missionaries, in cases where they are brought in contact with it, while seeking their one great object, therefore,

Resolved, That as this Board regard the system and practice of slaveholding as a great moral evil, entirely opposed to the

spirit and principles of the gospel whose propagation is its espe-
cial and appropriate work; it can never in the persons of its officers, agents, or missionaries, sustain any relation to it, implying
either approbation or sanction.

Resolved, That in accordance with this general principle, this
Board cannot appoint or sustain slaveholders, remaining such after remonstrance, as missionaries.

Resolved, That while this Board will not *imperatively* direct or
concern itself with the internal discipline of churches gathered
by its missionaries on heathen ground, as it might seem to be an
unauthorized interference with the liberty of Christ's house, so
neither can it allow such missionaries to interfere in a similar
way with its liberty in the appropriation of its funds; and therefore, that as this Board, in the exercise of its liberty, would feel
called upon to withdraw its support from missionaries and
churches receiving drunkards, gamblers, and the like to their
communion and retaining them in it, so it cannot continue its
appropriations to missionaries and churches which, after remon-
strances on the subject, deliberately continue to receive slaveholders remaining such after due admonition, to their bosom and
retain them in it.

Resolved, That the Board will expect its missionaries, minis-
tering to churches that have slaveholders in them, to pursue the
same course in respect to their instruction, admonition, and discipline as slaveholders, as if the same individuals were drunkards,
gamblers, or the like, and that if the missionaries, in the exercise
of their liberty and after full deliberation, shall decline to do so,
this Board hereby directs its Executive officers to dissolve farther
connection with them as missionaries of this body."

Of this Mr. Phelps, in a document since published
by him in his official capacity as Secretary of the
Anti-Slavery Society,* says:

" This, of course, as was our object in offering it, brought the
discussion to a point; and that point was simply this, viz.: whether in the matter of instruction, admonition, and discipline, the

---

* American and Foreign Anti-Slavery Reporter, October, 1845.

7*

Board would expect its missionaries and mission churches to treat slaveholding just as they would drunkenness, gaming, falsehood, idolatry, and the like. The report and the speakers had virtually said they would expect them to do so in respect to specific forms of maltreatment and personal abuse. The amendment raised the question whether they would expect them to do so in regard to slaveholding itself. In other terms, it raised the question whether slaveholding, as such, is to be classed with the other offences named, and whether so classed, instruction is to be given against it by missionaries, and admonition and discipline to be administered against it by them and the churches, in the same way, and only in the same, as in respect to said other offences."

This paragraph has its value, as showing that I do not misrepresent the actual question between the Anti-Slavery Society and the American Board. The question, according to Mr. Phelps' showing, is not a question respecting "specific forms of maltreatment." To condemn every specific wrong which the master may commit in the exercise of the power which the laws give him over his slaves, is not enough. To condemn him for buying and selling human beings as merchandise; to condemn him, in detail, for regarding and treating his servants as mere chattels; to condemn him for every particular act of wrong-doing towards them which convicts him of a selfish and unchristian heart; to condemn him for not duly recognizing their natural rights in the parental and conjugal relations, and for neglecting the necessities of their intellectual and moral nature, and their dignity as brethren of the human family, and as immortal beings to whom God speaks in the gospel—all this is not enough. The Anti-Slavery Society demands that he shall be condemned for the relation itself, without any inquiry touching his conduct in that relation. In the Anti-Slavery Society's creed, he that condemns a slave-owner only for well-defined individual acts of oppression, does the work of the Lord deceitfully; we are required to go back farther, and to condemn him for having the power to oppress.

Before taking leave of Mr. Phelps' paragraph above quoted, I cannot but remark, that the debate itself, as reported in the New York newspapers of that week, does not seem to correspond with his opinion that his motion to amend "brought the discussion to a point." The speeches prior to his motion—after a preliminary question, strangely raised, respecting the jurisdiction of the Board, had been cleared up—were as nearly to the point as those that followed. The issue presented in Mr. P.'s resolutions, is precisely the issue which was presented, under another form, in the report. The question discussed in the report, is not whether slavery is wrong as a political system, and is everywhere and necessarily mischievous; nor is it the question whether the treating of human beings as merchandise, or as having no personal rights, by those who happen to have the power of so doing, is wrong; it is simply the question whether the mere relation of a slave-owner is always and necessarily a crime, and as such incompatible with a Christian profession. That question the report answers in the negative; and it proposes, accordingly, that every individual instance of slave-ownership shall be judged in that respect by the missionaries and their churches. Mr. Phelps' amendment, on the contrary, gives to the same question an affirmative answer; and it proposes to instruct the missionaries everywhere, and the missionary churches, that the mere possession of a master's authority over a slave, independent of all specific exercise of that authority, is to be visited with excommunication. Mr. Phelps' motion, then, produced, and could produce, no effect on the course or progress of the debate, save as it may have helped to diminish the possibility of misunderstanding the demands of the Society which he represented.

It was my wish to finish all that I have to say respecting the late meeting of the Board at Brooklyn, in a single paper ; but I fear that in attempting to do so, I should occupy more space in the columns of the Evangelist, than would be consistent with the usual variety of matter in this widely read " folio of four pages." At this point, then, I pause, like a Congress orator suddenly struck down at the expiration of his hour. The present article may be considered as a statement and explanation of the question on which the Board was to act. In another article, I propose to offer some considerations on the decision of the Board, and the position in which it stands in respect to the Anti-Slavery Society.

NO. II.

THE ACTION OF THE BOARD.

The precise question before the Board should be distinctly remembered. It was not a question respecting that political institution which we call slavery. It was not a question whether acts of wrong-doing on the part of masters toward their servants, are inconsistent with Christian character and Christian communion. It was simply a question respecting the relation between a master and his slaves under the laws of a State which has incorporated the system of slavery among its political institutions; whether that relation, in itself, and without any specification of distinct acts of oppression committed by virtue of the power which the relation involves, is a crime for which the master should be cut off from communion with every Christian church. This was the question which the report from the Committee answered in the negative, and which Mr. Phelps' motion for amendment answered in the affirmative.

After the discussion had been prolonged till near the close of the second day, another amendment was moved by the writer of these papers, as a substitute for that proposed by Mr. Phelps. It was in these words:

"In conclusion, it seems proper for the Board, on this occasion, to put upon record a distinct assertion of the principles contained in the following resolutions:

1. *Resolved*, That inasmuch as the system of domestic slavery, under every modification, is at war with the principles of Christianity, with natural justice, with industry and thrift, with habits of subjection to law, and with whatever tends to the advancement of civilization and the ascendency of the gospel, and inasmuch as it brings upon every community which establishes and upholds it, the righteous displeasure of God, and the reprobation of the civilized and Christian world, the existence of slavery in the Cherokee and Choctaw nations is deeply to be lamented by their friends, and particularly by this Board, as hav-

ing been, for more than a quarter of a century, engaged in labors tending to their moral, intellectual, and social advancement.

2. *Resolved*, That while the strongest language of reprobation is not too strong to be applied to the system of slavery, truth and justice require this Board to say that the mere relation of a master to one whom the constitution of society has made a slave, is not to be regarded as in all cases such a sin as to require the exclusion of the master, without further inquiry, from Christian ordinances.

3. *Resolved*, That the missionaries of this Board, everywhere, are expected to admit to Christian ordinances those, and only those, who give satisfactory evidence of having become new creatures in Christ.

4. *Resolved*, That the master who buys and sells human beings, as merchandise, for gain—who does not recognize in respect to his servants the divine sanctity of their relations as husbands and wives, and as parents and children—who permits them to live and die in ignorance of God and of God's Word— who does not render to his servants that which is just and equal, or who refuses to recognize heartily and practically their dignity and worth, as reasonable and immortal beings, for whom Christ has died, does not give satisfactory evidence of being born of God, or having the spirit of Christ."

The reason. stated for moving this amendment was in effect, not that the report does not contain in some form of expression all that is contained in these resolutions, but that it seemed desirable to embody, in a formal series of propositions, or theses, a statement of what is and what is not to be condemned, making certain distinctions so definitely that all parties should see them, and, if possible, should be compelled to adopt them, or to dissent from them, without mystification. The first reso- . lution, accordingly, speaks of slavery as a political institution, and laments its introduction into the

nascent civilization of the Cherokee and Choctaw
nations; and thus it contradicts, on the one hand,
those who defend and uphold the institution of slavery, which is done by many at the South, and
which Dr. White was understood to do in that discussion—and on the other hand, those who stigma-
tize the Board, as defending and upholding slavery.
The second resolution denies peremptorily the peculiar dogma of the Anti-Slavery Society. The
third denies a principle assumed by some who hold
that a slave-owner may give undeniable evidence
of Christian character•notwithstanding his relation
to his slaves; but who insist that even in that case
he ought not to be admitted as a Christian to fellowship in Christian ordinances. The fourth points
out the legitimate, and only legitimate application
of church discipline against slavery, which is by
censuring and excommunicating the sinner, not for
having the power to do wrong, but for doing wrong
—not for standing in a certain constituted relation
toward his servants, but for his conduct toward them
in that relation.

This motion to amend was heartily seconded.
Nothing was said in opposition to it. But as the
second day of the debate was then closing, and as
the question before the house was becoming complicated with amendment upon amendment, it was
judged best to recommit the whole subject; and
accordingly the original report, and both the proposed amendments, were put into the hands of Chief
Justice Williams and five other gentlemen, one of
whom (Rev. John C. Webster) was himself one of
the memorialists. That Committee, the next morn-

ing, recommended the adoption of the original report without amendment. In the debate which followed there were some passages which I may be allowed to notice.

Immediately after the report had been made by Chief Justice Williams, with some explanations of the views of the Committee, the Rev. Dr. Tappan, who had served on both Committees, and who, I believe, not only claims the title of abolitionist, but has long been claimed by the Anti-Slavery Society as a patron, said, according to the summary of the debate given in the New-York Evangelist of that week,

" That every individual of the Committee approved of the principles of Dr. Bacon's resolutions, but it was feared that to append them to the report would look too much like legislation, and might seem to ecclesiastical bodies as if the Board was trenching upon their proper province. There are also other substantial reasons ; and though the report was believed to contain every principle contained in the resolutions, it was unadvisable to state them in this formal manner."

The American Board of Commissioners for Foreign Missions combines in one system of operations the foreign missionary charities of the New England Congregationalists, and the Constitutional (or New School) Presbyterians, and a respectable minority in the Old School body, and of the Reformed Dutch Church. The ecclesiastical bodies of New England have no such jealousy as that referred to by Dr. Tappan. Had the resolutions been adopted, no Association, no Conference, no church or council of churches, from Madawasca to Horseneck, would

have suspected that the Board was going one hair's
breadth out of its proper province. In the Presbyterian connection (New School) there might be
some danger, but not much, of wakening that jealousy. The Dutch Church, however, conducts its
foreign missionary operations in connection with
the American Board, through an auxiliary board of
its own, which is under the control of its ecclesiastical judicatories. In that body, therefore, characterized as it is by a large, though not disreputable,
share of the ecclesiastical spirit, some jealousy
might easily be excited by any ill-considered proceeding. Much deference is due to the judgment,
and even to the prejudices, of such men as represent
the Dutch Church in the American Board of Foreign
Missions, and in other kindred institutions. If those
men should say to me that the report in its original
form would be highly satisfactory to them and to
their brethren, and that the report with these resolutions appended would be likely to waken some
jealousy on the part of their judicatories, and to
retard the progress of missionary zeal in their congregations, I should feel at once that an element
not before contemplated was to be taken into calcu-
lation; and that whatever advantages would result
from the amendment in one direction, might be
counterbalanced by the disadvantages in another
quarter. Just so, if men perfectly acquainted with
the state of the missions to the Choctaws and with
the dangers which beset the missionaries, should
tell me that the report in its original form would be
safe in respect to any use that would be likely to be
made of it by wicked men with the design of break-

ing up the missions, but that the resolutions might
be employed by malicious white men to embarrass
the missionaries in their relation to the political
authorities of the Choctaw nation, and to procure
their expulsion from the field; then, though the *ruat
cœlum* abolitionists might cry out, So much the better !—let the missions be broken up !—let the missionaries be murdered !—and might insist that the
prospect of such results was the best of all reasons
for putting the decision of the Board into this precise form ;—my sense of duty would constrain me
to hesitate long before determining, in the face of
such a risk, to sum up the principles and reasonings
of the report in those resolutions at the end. I can
conceive, therefore, of very good reasons why the
Committee unanimously agreeing in the principles
asserted by those resolutions, might deem it unne-
cessary and unwise to express those principles in
that particular form. And to any reader who cares
to know what my opinion was as a member of that
Committee, I may say that though my own mind
was not fully convinced that any considerable harm
was likely to result from the adoption of my amendment, I could, and did, acquiesce in the decision of
the majority.

After Dr. Tappan's speech, the Rev. Mr. Webster said, that he found himself compelled, with
great reluctance, to differ from his colleagues of the
Committee, and claimed the privilege of presenting
" a minority report," which he proceeded to offer in
the form of a speech.* I subjoin the sketch of his

---

* I know not why it should not be stated that in the Committee
Mr. W. did not vote against the report—did not give any intimation of

ᵣᴜmarks given by the reporters for the New York Evangelist.

"It was from no want of attachment to the Board, on the contrary it was because he loved the Board, and because he desired this perplexing qnestion to be settled in such a way as to promote harmony of feeling, that he could not assent to the report as it is. He would have been satisfied with Dr. Bacon's resolutions; and if all the principles of the resolutions were contained in the report, he saw no good reason why they should not be frankly summed up at the close. This would have satisfied all parties. As it is, he feared that a large number of the Board's best friends would not be satisfied. The general impression will be that although slavery is condemned, there is a loop-hole left for all who love to hold slaves."

I cannot but call attention distinctly to the positions taken by Mr. Webster as a dissentient member of the Committee. He expressly gives up the Anti-Slavery dogma. "*He would have been satisfied with Dr. Bacon's resolutions,*" which contain a deliberate and formal denial of the distinctive doctrine of the Anti-Slavery Society, and which were proposed avowedly for the purpose—though not for the exclusive purpose—of uttering that denial. Nay, he speaks not for himself only, but for his party. "This," he says—that is, the addition of the resolu-

---

an intention to offer a minority report—nay, expressly said that he wished to be understood as voting neither for the report nor against it. It was, therefore, with some surprise that his "colleagues" of the Committee found him, in the morning, in the attitude of positive opposition to the decision towards which, in the evening, his attitude had been that of passive acquiescence. His right to change his mind after communing with his own heart on his bed, is undoubted; but it seems to me that so formal and unusual a step as that of offering a "minority report" ought not to have been taken without giving notice to the majority of the Committee, or at least as much notice as might be implied in a vote against their decision.

tions as an amendment to the report—" *this would have satisfied all parties.*" His opposition to the report in the original form, is because it does not go so far as that amendment. " The general impression will be, that although slavery is condemned, there is a loop-hole left for all who love to hold slaves." The amendment, then, in his judgment, would have prevented this impression. I have no doubt that Mr. Webster was honest in this; that he spoke as he felt. Nor have I any doubt that many anti-slavery men of the same kind felt as he did, and verily thought that they would have been satisfied with my resolutions.

Mr. Phelps, however, held his ground with unflinching logical consistency. I might perhaps make one exception to this remark. There was a moment when truth seemed to be breaking into his mind through the thick drapery of sophisms which he weaves so skillfully, but it was only a moment. He made no such admissions as those into which Mr. Webster was led by his less practiced ingenuousness. The Anti-Slavery Society would have been in a sorry plight, had its Secretary been so inconsequent in his reasonings as to profess himself satisfied with a resolution declaring that the mere relation of a master to his slaves is not necessarily a crime on the part of the master. Accordingly, Mr. P. embraced that last opportunity to reassert his one great principle in a speech, and in a new motion to amend the report. His second motion for amendment was in effect the same with the first. It proposed to make the report declare, in conclusion, that " the Board will expect its missionaries to treat slaveholding, in the matter of instruction, admonition and discipline, in the same manner as they should and would treat drunkenness, gaming, falsehood, bigamy, idolatry and the like; and that whenever and wherever it shall appear that the missionaries and the churches, in the exercise of their appropriate liberty, do not do so, it will be the duty of this Board, in the exercise of its liberty, to dissolve farther connection with them." The amendment was rejected without farther discussion; and the original report, as is well known, was adopted by a unanimous vote of the corporation, including seventy-five individuals there present, from every denomination represented in the Board, and of almost every shade of opinion in those various denominations. Some of those votes, it should be remembered, were given by men who have gloried in being abolitionists, who have co-operated in anti-slavery meetings and measures, and whose names have been—and are now—a tower of strength to the Anti-Slavery Society.

I now propose to show that the report, as it came from the Committee, and as it was adopted by the Board, does contain everything that was contained in those resolutions which, Mr. Webster assures us, would have satisfied, not only him as one of the memorialists, but "all parties." The most convenient and conclusive method of doing this, is by putting the language of the resolutions and the language of the report, upon each of the four topics, side by side.

The first topic is, *slavery as a political system, and as introduced into the Cherokee and Choctaw nations.*

What do the resolutions say? What says the report?

Resolution.—" Inasmuch as the *system* of domestic slavery, under every modification, is at war with the principles of Christianity, with natural justice, with industry and thrift, with habits of subjection to law, and with whatever tends to the advancement of civilization and the ascendency of the gospel; and inasmuch as it brings upon every community which establishes and upholds it, the righteous displeasure of God, and the reprobation of the civilized and Christian world; the existence of slavery in the Cherokee and Choctaw nations, is deeply to be lamented by their friends, and particularly by this Board, as having been for more than a quarter of a century engaged in labors tending to their moral, intellectual and social advancement."

Report.—" The Committee do not deem it necessary to discuss the general subject of slavery, as it exists in these United States, or to enlarge on *the wickedness of the system,* or on *the disastrous moral and social influences* which slavery exerts upon the less enlightened and less civilized communities where the missionaries of this Board are laboring. On *these* points, there is probably, among the members of the Board and its friends, little difference of opinion."

Again: " The *unrighteousness of the principles on which the whole system is based, and the violation of the rights of man, the debasement, wickedness and misery it involves, and which, in fact, are witnessed* to a greater or less extent *wherever it exists, must call forth the hearty condemnation* of all possessed of

Christian feeling and sense of right, and make its *entire and speedy removal* an object of earnest and prayerful desire to every true friend of God and man."

Again: "Wherever the gospel is brought to bear upon the community where slavery or any other form of oppression exists, *its spirit is decidedly adverse to such a state of things.*"

Again: "That slavery should exist at all in those tribes, (Cherokee and Choctaw,) who have suffered so severely from the violation of their own rights by their white neighbors, is deeply to be regretted; and all should earnestly pray that as social improvement and Christian knowledge are rapidly advancing among them, they may *speedily* and nobly exemplify the spirit of true philanthropy, as well as the gospel law of love, by showing that they duly appreciate the rights and welfare of the whole race of man."

Further: "The Committee cannot advert to some of the laws enacted by both the Cherokees and Choctaws, without pain and regret, especially those which prohibit teaching slaves to read, throw impediments in the way of emancipation, restrict slaves in the possession of property, and embarrass the residence of free negroes among them." "Slavery was introduced among these Indians, and has been regulated by them, in *unhappy imitation of their white neighbors in the adjacent States.*"

Once more: " *Viewed in all its bearings, it is a* TREMENDOUS EVIL. Its destructive influence is seen on the *morals* of the master and slave. It sweeps away those barriers which every civilized community has erected to protect *the purity and chastity of the family relations.*" "A great proportion of the red people who own slaves, neglect entirely to train their children to *habits of industry, enterprise and economy,* so necessary in forming the character of the parent and the citizen. *Slavery,* so far as it extends, *will ever present formidable obstacles to the right training of the rising generation.*"

So much for the agreement of the resolutions and the report on the subject matter of the first resolution. The second topic is the *distinction* between the wrongfulness of slavery as a political institution, and the responsibility of the individual master for the existence of the relation between him and those whom that unnatural and unjust system has placed under him ; or, in other words, *the distinction between slavery as a system and slaveholding as a relation constituted by that system ;* and, as a corollary from this plain distinction, the *denial of the Anti-Slavery Society's dogma,* which is held only by resolutely blinking this distinction. How far do the resolutions and the report agree on this point. Let them speak.

Resolution.—"While the strongest language of reprobation is not too strong to be applied to the *system* of slavery, truth and justice require this Board to say that the mere *relation* of a master to one whom the constitution of society has made a slave, is not to be regarded as, in all cases, such a sin as to require the exclusion of the master, without farther inquiry, from Christian ordinances."

Report.—"Strongly as your committee are convinced of the wrongfulness and evil tendencies of

slaveholding, and ardently as they desire its speedy
and universal termination, still they cannot think
that, in all cases, it involves individual guilt in such
a manner, that every individual implicated in it can
on Scriptural grounds be excluded from Christian
fellowship. In the language of Dr. Chalmers, when
treating on this point in a recent letter, the Committee would say, '*Distinction ought to be made between the character of a system, and the character of
the persons whom circumstances have implicated there-
with,*' " &c. "Slavery (says he) we hold to be a
system chargeable with atrocities and evils often the
most hideous and appalling which have either af-
flicted or deformed our species ; yet we must not say
of every man born within its territory—who by inheritance is himself the owner of slaves—that unless
he make the resolute sacrifice, and renounce his
property in slaves, he is therefore not a Christian,
and should be treated as an outcast from all the distinctions and privileges of Christian society."

If on this point there is any difference between
the resolutions and the report, it is that the latter is
more anti-slavery than the former. The report sometimes, like the Anti-Slavery Society, uses the word
"slaveholding" as synonomous with " slavery ;"
and it seems to take for granted the idea that the
mere ownership of slaves always implies, in whatever circumstances, some degree of criminality on the
part of the owner, and is so much detracted from the
evidence of his Christian character. In the language
quoted from Dr. Chalmers, it seems to be implied
that though the master of slaves may peradventure
be a passably good man, notwithstanding that unfor -

8

tunate relation, still if he were only a better man—
if he had a little more of Christian principle—he
would cease to stand in that relation; whereas, my
doctrine—though I confess that in that hastily drafted
resolution, it is not so amply and distinctly stated as
it should have been—reaches to the extent of admitting the possibility of a case in which the man's intelligent and deliberate consenting to stand in the
relation of a master to those whom the law has
made his slaves, his holding and executing instead
of renouncing, the trust which the State, under a barbarous constitution of society, has put into his hands,
shall be a brighter and more conclusive evidence of
his disinterestedness and Christian integrity, than he,
in those circumstances, could achieve by any act of
manumission.

The third topic is *the denial of all tests of church
communion which are not also tests of spiritual regeneration.* On this point, let the resolution speak, as
before, and then the report.

Resolution.—"The missionaries of the Board,
everywhere, are expected to admit to Christian ordinances, *those, and only those who give satisfactory
evidence of having become new creatures in Christ.*"

Report.—" As the ordinances of baptism and the
Lord's Supper are obviously designed by Christ to be
means of grace for *all who give credible evidence of
repentance and faith* in Him, these ordinances cannot
scripturally and rightfully be denied to professed
converts from among the heathen after they shall
have given such evidence."

Again: " On this principle of receiving to their
churches all those, and only those, who give satisfac-

tory evidence of repentance and faith in the Lord Jesus Christ, they [the missionaries] all appear to have proceeded."

The fourth topic is *the proper application of church discipline in respect to slavery.* On this subject the dictate of common sense is that the master who exercises his legal power over his servants to do them wrong, is to be censured, not indeed for having the power to do wrong with legal impunity, but for the specific wrong-doing.

Resolution.—"The master who buys and sells human beings, as merchandise, for gain; who does not recognize, in respect to his servants, the divine sanctity of their relation as husbands and wives, and as parents and children; who permits them to live and die in ignorance of God and of God's Word; who does not render to his servants that which is just and equal; or who refuses to recognize, heartily and practically, their dignity and worth as reasonable and immortal beings, for whom Christ has died; does not give satisfactory evidence of being born of God, or having the spirit of Christ."

Report.—"Should any church member who has servants under him, be chargeable with *cruelty,* IN-JUSTICE *or* UNKINDNESS *towards them,* should he neglect what is essential to their *present comfort or their eternal welfare;* or should he *in any manner transgress the particular instructions which the apostles give* concerning the conduct of a master, he would be *admonished* by the church, and unless he should repent, he would be *excommunicated.*"

Again: "In respect to the kind and amount of instruction given by the missionaries, in relation to slavery and the duties of masters and slaves, the missionaries seem substantially to agree. Mr. Byington says, 'We give such instructions to masters and servants as are contained in the epistles.' 'In private we converse about all the evils and dangers of slavery.' Of a similar tenor are the remarks of Mr. Wright. 'The instructions, public and private, direct and indirect, have been such as are found in the Bible.' "

On this point, then, either the report is entirely unworthy of credit, as a representation of facts, or any master in a church under the care of our missionaries, who should be convicted of any of the specifications set down in the resolution, "would be admonished by the church; and unless he should repent, he would be excommunicated." And in the name of justice—nay, in the name of Christ, whose honor is so deeply implicated in this matter—I demand that the contrary shall not be asserted or assumed as the basis of argument against the missionaries or the Board, without clear proof.

If any man, then, shall venture to affirm that there are masters in our Cherokee and Choctaw churches, who buy and sell human beings, as merchandise, for gain—who do not recognize the divine sanctity of the relations of husbands and wives, parents and children, among their servants—who permit their servants to live and die in ignorance of God and of God's Word—who do not render to their servants that which is just and equal—or who refuse to recognize their dignity and worth as reasonable and immortal beings for whom Christ has died—I demand of that man that he shall identify the church and the offender; that he shall, in the presence of that church convict that offender, not of sustaining the relation of a master, but of some of these specific wrong-doings; and that, having done this, he shall bring back a well-authenticated statement to show that the church, with the specifications distinctly proved, refused to censure the offender. If he will not, or cannot, do this, let him confess himself a calumniator of God's people.

At the risk of being tedious, I must ask two questions, in view of the comparison which I have thus instituted between the resolutions presented by myself and the report adopted by the Board.

First, How was it possible for Mr. Phelps, with all his perspicacity, to say, as he says in the manifesto from which I made a quotation last week :

"The anti-slavery sentiments expressed by such men as Messrs. Bacon, Hawes, Beecher, Stowe, Dwight, &c., are not to be taken as defining at all the actual position of the Board. They are the sentiments of individuals. They did not prevail in the Board. On the contrary, the Board distinctly rejected the resolutions of Dr. Bacon, which were a summary expression of them. The Board, therefore, is no more to have the credit of them than it is to have the credit of the sentiments expressed by Dr. Ide and other abolitionists, and embodied in our amendments. It is no more to have the credit of them than the curse of what was uttered by the slaveholder, Elipha White, and his worthy compeer, Dr. Wisner. It is to have neither the credit, nor the curse of either, but must stand and be judged solely on what it did and what it refused to do—on the report adopted, and the amendments rejected."

The Board did *not* "distinctly reject" the resolutions proposed by me. In regard to those resolutions, the Board took no distinct vote, except the vote by which they were referred to a committee. The question of adopting or rejecting them was never put. The only amendment "rejected," was Mr. Phelps' second amendment. So far as any "anti-slavery sentiments expressed by such men as Messrs. Bacon, Hawes, Beecher, Stowe, Dwight, &c.," were 'summarily expressed' in my resolutions, they are all expressed, as I have shown, not indeed more summarily, but more fully, and with even more of a technically anti-slavery tone, in the report adopted by the Board. I am far from imputing to Mr. Phelps any intentional misrepresentation. I only suppose, that in the singleness of his devotion to the cause of his society, he did not examine, so carefully as he should have examined, the facts that lay in the printed documents before him.

Secondly, Is it not plain that those who would have been "satisfied" with the adoption of the resolutions proposed by me, ought to be satisfied, if they are reasonable men, with the report as it stands? Is it not plain that, in lending their voices to a clamor against the Board, as if those resolutions contained something which the report, as adopted, does not contain, they will put themselves into a position in which they must appear very much like tools in the hands of other men? Those men who would have been thus "satisfied," will find a much better guide in their own instinctive common sense, and their love of substantial and practicable usefulness, than in the transcendental formulæ of the Anti-Slavery Society, or the movements of its Executive Committee.

NO. III.

WHAT HAS CHURCH GOVERNMENT TO DO WITH SLAVERY?—
WHAT IS SLAVERY IN THE UNITED STATES?

Immediately after the publication of the first of these articles, I received a friendly letter from Mr. Phelps, representing that I omit all notice of what he deems an important qualification of his position. An extract from his letter, and a brief explanation of my views in regard to it, may serve as an introduction to what I propose to say on another part of the general subject:

"My position, then, allow me to say, is just this, that the mere fact of slaveholding, in the same way and in the same sense, as the mere fact of drunkenness, falsehood, or gaming, is (1) to constitute the ground and occasion for instruction, public or private, or both, against it; (2) that such instruction resisted, and the thing persevered in, are to be the ground and occasion for admonition, or the commencement in some way of religious discipline; and (3) that instruction and admonition both resisted, and the thing still persevered in, are to constitute the ground and occasion for excommunication. This I hold to be the *general rule*, admitting possibly of exceptions, but of none save such as could be admitted in regard to the other cases named, and on the same proof or grounds as in respect to them. And this I hold not on the alone ground of the sinfulness of slaveholding in all cases (though I believe that), but on the broader, and what might be the *common*, ground of all parties, that it is justly, in this day, an occasion of reproach and an appearance of evil from which every follower of Christ is bound, at all hazards, to abstain—in other words, that if not sinful in itself, it is, to quote the Presb. Book of Discipline, something ' in the principles or practice' of a man, fitted to ' tempt others to sin, and mar their spiritual edification'—not, in a word, *walking orderly*.

The point, however, to which I wish particularly to call your attention, is that of instruction and admonition *previous* to excommunication—making the final excision not for the mere fact itself, but for the fact persevered in against such instruction and admonition. In this view, the mere fact is not excision. It only raises the question of character and becomes the occasion and ground for instruction. It *puts the man on the proof of his character*. That is all. If he can prove his case an exception to the general rule, very well; then, just as in the other cases, let him stand in the church, not according to the rule, but a confessed, and everywhere understood, exception to it."

Mr. Phelps assures me that he regards this " qualification of his position," for so he calls it, as " very important." But I must confess it does not strike me as affecting at all the position which he and the Anti-Slavery Society are understood to hold. If anybody had imputed to Mr. Phelps and his colleagues an intention of " exscinding" all slaveholders from the church, in violation of all the rules and forms of church discipline, as an accidental majority in the Presbyterian Assembly of 1837 " exscinded" some 60,000 church members in Western New York and Northern Ohio—then this qualification of his position would have been important. In reference to the actual question, the " qualification" is altogether irrelevant. The question is not whether the master of a slave shall have the privilege of being instructed and admonished, privately, and by the church, (according to Christ's precept, Matt. xviii. 15–17,) before the final sentence of excommunication; but whether the admonition shall be for the mere fact that he sustains the relation of a master, or for the very different fact that in the exercise of the power which that relation confers upon him he has been guilty of some specific injustice toward the slave. Mr. Phelps' position is, that the relation itself is the crime—that the man is to be admonished for having the *power* to do wrong—that if, under admonition, he does not repent and "bring forth fruits meet for repentance," by immediately abdicating that power "*at all hazards*," he is to be excommunicated. The only exceptions to this rule which he would admit, are such exceptions as would be admitted in regard to drunkenness, falsehood and gaming. In other words, there is to be *no exception ;* for that Mr. Phelps can imagine a case in which a drunkard, a liar, or a gamester, who refuses to repent and reform after due instruction and admonition, ought not to be excommunicated, is what my respect for him will not permit me to believe.

To prevent any misunderstanding it seems proper to say expressly, that Mr. Phelps' letter was written with no view to publication, and with no intention of engaging in a reply to these articles of mine. I have made this quotation—not without first asking and obtaining his permission—because I knew not in what other way I could so properly render what he regards as justice to him. I have added the explanation of my own views because it seemed no more than justice to myself.

Dismissing, then, this mutual explanation between Mr. Phelps and myself, I proceed to consider more distinctly the general question which has come up between the Anti-Slavery Society and the Board of Missions, and which is urged as a practical question upon all the churches in the United States. What is the natural and legitimate action of Christianity

8*

against slavery ?   What should be done on this subject by the churches, administering and applying
the principles of Christianity to determine the question of the visible Christian character of individuals
claiming recognition of Christ's followers?   In other
words : What has church government to do with
slavery?

Let us take this question as it actually arises in
the United States.   Let us look at " slavery as it is"
in our own country, where after all we have far
more to do with it than we have to do with slavery
in any other country.   It may be presumed that
when we have answered the question in relation to
our own country, so as to be sure that our answer
rests upon the right *principles*, it will be easy enough
to answer the same question in regard to any other
country.

In fifteen of the twenty-eight States of this Union,
there exists in the structure of society a certain artificial relation between man and man, a relation of
power on the one hand and of dependence and subjection on the other, which is the subject matter of
our present inquiry.   The population of those States
is divided into two great classes, the free and the
enslaved, with a smaller intermediate class which,
under the established policy of most of those States,
is rapidly diminishing.   The free are those of un-
mixed European blood, or of what passes for such.
The enslaved are of another race ; the great majority
being of pure African descent, and those of mixed
blood being counted with their African kindred.   A
few of the enslaved race have acquired an imperfect
and precarious freedom hedged in with various dis-

abilities, and they constitute an anomalous class between the bond and the free.

The theory of society in all that portion of the Union, is that the state consists only of one class, the free; and that the enslaved race have no rights, no being, as members of the body politic. The state is considered as having its existence in and for its white inhabitants only. Laws are enacted, magistrates are chosen, justice is administered, society itself exists, not with the remotest reference to the welfare of the negro as an end, but only for the protection and the interests of that part of the population which belongs to what naturalists call " the Caucasian variety" of the human species. If certain forms and degrees of cruelty are prohibited by the laws, it is not on the ground that the negro has any human rights, but only as " cruelty to animals" is prohibited by the laws of every civilized community, because it is offensive to human sensibilities, and because it tends to brutalize the temper and manners of the people. The theory of society there regards the black population as *in* the state but not *of* it. The state does nothing for their improvement or elevation; it cares not for their morals; it takes no cognizance of any of their wants as human beings. With the inconsiderable exception of the anomalous class of free blacks, it knows them only as property like other cattle. In the theory of society—in the laws—and generally in the administration of law—they are regarded not at all as persons, but only as chattels. In Virginia, I believe, and perhaps under some other jurisdictions, the state does not even hang a negro for murdering his master, without first buying him of the master's heirs, and so making him public property for that public use.

Accordingly, the law, throughout those States, presumes every black man to be somebody's property, till his exemption from the rule is made out by positive evidence; just as elsewhere every horse, every cow, every pig is presumed to have an owner, and whoever pretends to be the owner is so unless another claimant appears with superior evidence of legal ownership. In most of those slave States, the most stringent regulations make it well nigh impossible for a slave to become a freeman; and generally the free individuals of the enslaved race were made free long ago, before the present policy was fully established. If a master abdicates his power over his slave, the state concerns itself immediately to put that slave under another master, by requiring the sheriff to sell him *sub hasta*.

In other words, the structure of society throughout that portion of the Union is such, that the state refuses to take the African population under its protection or government. That entire moiety of the population the state regards not as citizens, nor even as its own subjects, but only as property belonging to citizens. It insists that every black shall have a master, as his proprietor, and therefore his protector and governor; it guaranties to the master all the physical force necessary to keep his slaves in subjection; it allows him to inflict almost any punishment short of death at his own discretion; it interferes between him and his slaves only to prevent certain extreme cruelties on the one hand, and on the other to forbid those acts of indulgence and beneficence which are considered inconsistent with the permanence and security of the system. For all that protection which every subject has a right to expect from the government that is set over him, and for nearly all that salutary control which it is the business of civil government to exert over the actions of its subjects, the black man must look not to the state, but to his master. The master upon his plantation is a petty monarch, with the powers of an African or Oriental despot; the negroes upon his soil are his subjects. If he needs a military force to suppress an insurrection of his subjects, or to compel their obedience, the state comes to his aid. If one of his slaves commits some crime particularly dangerous not to him only or to his plantation, but to the public considered as consisting of white men, the state takes the work of trial and punishment into its own hands. If his administration of his power becomes in certain particulars too oppressive, or in certain particulars too lax and beneficent, the state counteracts that " evil example " by the infliction of penalties upon him. If he abdicates his power, the state will commit that power to some other person. The state considers the blacks as a barbarous hostile population which it utterly refuses to take under its protection; and it tolerates their existence within its boundaries only on the condition that all the most essential duties of government, in respect to them, shall be performed by individuals sustaining towards them the relation of proprietorship.

Such is the system of society—the structure and

arrangement of civil relations—which in fifteen of these United States is established under the name of slavery. The institution is entirely and essentially barbarous. No form of government on earth is more at war with every just conception of the nature of man and of his rights as a member of society. All that I know of the ordinary operation of this form of government, in its influence on industry, on morals, on all the interests of the individual and of the commonwealth, is in harmony with its theory. And in proportion to the progress of civilization among the enslaved portion of society, the intrinsic wickedness of that mode of government becomes more glaringly evident, and more offensive to the moral sensibilities of mankind. The system of arrangements for the government of the negroes was established long ago, when the ancestors of those negroes, captured in the ambushes and fights of hostile tribes on the banks of the Zaire and the Gambia, were introduced by crowded shiploads into dependent and feeble colonies under the relentless legislation of the mother country. In that age those arrangements might have seemed to be excused by the plea that there was no other way of dealing with savages so desperate, under the sense of recent enslavement, and so ignorant even of the language of their masters; though even then they must have been condemned, by a thoughtful sense of justice, as inexcusable. But now the atrocity of those arrangements stands out in strong relief against the sky before the gazing world; for now the negroes are as native to the soil as their masters; and notwithstanding that tyrannical opposition to their improvement and progress which is kept up by the state and generally by the individual masters, they are slowly but steadily rising towards a level with the superior race in all the essentials of civilization, and are already as unlike the barbarians that were brought from Africa, as the high-bred Virginian lady, than whom, perhaps, there lives no specimen of womanhood more admirable, is unlike her fair ancestor, warranted "incorrupt," who was sold to a planter husband some two hundred and thirty years ago, for one hundred and twenty pounds of tobacco.

The question before us is not whether the political system which puts the black population of the southern States into the power of individual masters, absolute and irresponsible, and which studiously withholds from them all human rights, is consistent with the law of God. Nor is it the question whether the free people of those States, in their sovereignty, ought to enter at once upon the long-neglected work of reforming their barbarous institutions. Nor are we to inquire here respecting the duty of the slave—whether he owes any allegiance to the state which refuses to protect him or to recognize him as a man—whether in all circumstances he retains the right which our national legislation, our diplomacy, and our last war with Great Britain have challenged for all mankind, the right of expatriating himself and renouncing his allegiance to the government under which he was born—whether, or in what circumstances, he may rise up with his brethren in bondage to throw off the yoke, to assert their freedom, and to form a new constitution. Nor have I any occasion here to answer the question whether I may rightfully give shelter, and food, and clothing to a fugitive from Virginia, and money to help him on his way to Jamaica or to Canada.* The only question is, What has Christianity to do with the reformation of this whole order of things, which is known by the name of slavery? And, in particular, what has Christianity, in the form of church government, to do in the business of setting right the wrongs of so wicked a system of social order?

One of the embarrassments incident to this mode of communicating with the public, is the necessity of breaking up a discussion of an important and complicated subject into weekly chapters, and thus separating parts that ought to be presented in close

---

* An anonymous friend, who writes to me from New York, says, "At this moment, I am called upon to aid a poor fugitive with his wife and five children, who have escaped the *mere relation*, having arrived from Virginia last evening. As this is a case of frequent occurrence, will Dr. Bacon please to indicate my duty in the next Evangelist?"

The proposer of this case of conscience is probably capable of seeing that his question has no bearing whatever on the subject of the present discussion. Yet, that I may not seem to treat even the writer of an anonymous letter with neglect, I will answer his question frankly. If a "fugitive with his wife and five children" were to come to me with the confession that he had run away from the *mere relation* of servitude, and not from any unkind, oppressive or unchristian *treatment* on the part of his master, and should ask me to help him with money, I should probably esteem *that* fugitive a shiftless vagabond; I should tell him that by his own showing he had no occasion to run away, and that if he had expressed a reasonable desire to emigrate to some other country, his master would doubtless have put him in the way of helping himself instead of depending on charity: and I should probably reserve my sympathy and my aid for those fugitives who run away from actual and specific oppression. And if I should find that the case of this fugitive from the *mere* relation of servitude is "a case of frequent occurrence," I should think much better of the masters, and much worse of the slaves, than I now do.

connection with each other. But to this disadvantage I submit, for the sake of speaking to thousands at once. The further discussion of the question, this week, would make too long an article. I can only indicate, as with a word, the intended course of the discussion, asking the reader to wait patiently till he is sure he understands me.

What has Christianity—what has the church to do with slavery? *Nothing*—and yet *everything*. In one sense—in one mode of action—*nothing*. In another sense, and by another kind of influence, *everything*.

NO. IV.

WHAT HAS CHURCH GOVERNMENT TO DO WITH SLAVERY?

The question respecting what Christianity, and particularly the Christian church, has to do with forms of civil government, and with those relations of man to man which exist in the structure of society—is, at the present day, at least as important as the question respecting what the state has to do with Christianity. What the state has to do with the church, is pretty well understood in this country, and is in the way to be understood throughout the world. What the church has to do with the state is not, in all quarters, so well understood. And yet, is it not self-evident that if, as we hold, the state is to let the church alone, the church on the other hand must let the state alone? The views which I have been led to entertain on this subject, are submitted to the public with diffidence, as my contribution to the discussion of a great and comprehensive question.

Moses, as God's messenger to a chosen race, established, in the name of God, a system not of morals merely, nor of religion, but of political order and government. There is no religious institution in the Old Testament which is not also political. Lessons of morality, and of faith and devotion, not only in the Pentateuch, but generally in the Scriptures of that dispensation, are given in the closest combination with national history and municipal regulations. The idea of a church distinct from the civil state is not in the Old Testament. Consequently, the system of the Old Testament was a system incapable of extension in the world. It was constructed for one nation only, and could not be imparted to another. It was designed not for man as man, but only for man as an Israelite in the land of Israel; and he, of any other race, who would embrace the system and enjoy all its privileges, must renounce his country and nation and become an Israelite by adoption. The reasons of this divine arrangement would be an interesting subject of inquiry; but the *fact* is all that concerns us at present.

The Old Testament, then, is a political book; as really so, though not as exclusively, as the Federalist, or Hallam's Constitutional History. Is the New Testament, in this respect, like the Old? Does the New Testament contain anything of the nature of civil regulation? Does it lay down any principle or rule with reference to political subjects, such as the structure of the state, the liberty of the individual members of society, the distribution of political powers, the responsibility of rulers to the people ;—or does it take all these things as it finds them, and leave them, as it leaves the physical sciences and arts, to take their chance with the general progress of human improvement ? Did Christ set himself up—was he announced by his apostles—as a legislator for society, and a reformer of political institutions ? On the contrary, is it not one of the most wonderful of the divine wonders in the character and history of our Saviour, that, pressed as he was on every side by the politicians of that day, Pharisees, Herodians, Sadducees; by all the national feelings and impulses of the Jewish people, and by the universally understood identity of politics and religion—he so carefully and skillfully avoided committing himself on any political question whatever. Is not the same thing in the conduct of the apostles, and the primitive churches under their direction, almost equally wonderful? Christ's kingdom, as announced by himself and his apostles, was not of this world. The church had nothing to do with the social or political relations of its members. It had no concern with any movement towards the re-organization of society.

I do not suppose that I am propounding a novelty, or that what I am now saying is likely to be contradicted by any for whom I write. And yet I would have the reader dwell upon this peculiarity of Christianity and of the Christian church, till he shall see it with the same sense of its importance which has been impressed upon my mind. The

New Testament shows us no Moses, standing before Pharaoh to demand the emancipation of an oppressed people—no Joshua, conquering a land of promise and dividing it among the conquerors—no Samuel, framing' new constitutions, and anointing kings in God's name. But it shows us Paul in chains, now reasoning with Felix, now answering before Nero; and Jesus of Nazareth, at the bar of Pilate, testifying to the truth, and declaring, " My kingdom is not of this world." Had Pilate been converted, would Christ have required him to throw up his commission of procurator of Judea? Had Nero been converted, would Paul, before admitting him to baptism, have required him to abdicate his imperial power, and to leave the nations of the Roman empire to constitute themselves, if they could, into a great federal union of free republics?

The system of the New Testament is, therefore, capable of universal extension. It addresses itself not to sovereigns or states as such, prescribing to them new laws and political institutions, and summoning them to launch upon the sea of revolution, but to individuals, calling them to repentance. All that it demands of states and governments, as such, is toleration for itself—" freedom to worship God." Thus it goes out into all the world, preaching to every creature that will hear, commanding all men everywhere to repent, and leaving all political relations and institutions to adjust themselves as they may—and as under God's providence they must —to that altered state of things which exists wherever the gospel prevails.

This is not only a distinction between Christianity and the system of the Old Testament; it is equally a distinction between Christianity and all the schemes of human wisdom for the redemption of the world from misery. St. Simonism, Fourierism, Socialism, and all other *isms* of that kind, propose the re-organization of society as their object; for they regard all the evil that is in the world as the effect of bad systems of government, bad laws, bad social arrangements; and they, therefore, have no doubt that human nature will do well enough if it can be relieved from the pressure of disadvantageous circumstances. Christianity bears no resemblance to these projects. It simply proposes to make *men* better—individual men—by inspiring them with new ideas and new principles of action, so that instead of being selfish they shall be benevolent, and instead of wronging and oppressing one another they shall recognize each other as brethren, and delight to do each other good; and it leaves these new ideas and principles to work out their own effects upon the structure of society.

Christianity, then, at the beginning, as announced by Christ himself and his apostles, had nothing to do in the way of interference with politics and legislation. It did not undertake to reform or change any man's condition as a member of society. And yet that gospel which we find in the sermon on the mount, in the Epistle to the Romans, in the story of the crucifixion, was destined, and was in one sense designed, to effect the greatest changes in the structure of society throughout the world. In the ideas and principles proclaimed by Christ and his apostles, and put on record in the Scriptures of the New

Testament, there came into the world a power, the progress of which from age to age, and from land to land, is the path of revolution. "Behold," saith God in reference to the diffusion and victories of the gospel—"Behold I make all things new." The kingdom which is not of this world was destined to change the world that knows it not ; as the changes of unconscious nature, the tides, the winds, the seasons with their bloom and their decay, are all effected by influences that are not of earth, but radiate from other spheres. The propagation of those ideas which constitute the gospel, their progressive ascendency in the minds of men, their dominion over the public sentiment of nations and of the world, was to work out in the end the universal re-organization of society—the recognition of the brotherhood of all mankind as the only just basis of legislation—the abolition of all unrighteous laws and of all those institutions founded on force and maintained by fraud, which withhold from labor its due recompense—the annihilation of all artificial restrictions upon industry and commerce—the breaking of every yoke of bondage—the subversion of every aristocracy and every throne.

To some readers, all this may seem entirely aside from the subject in hand. I feel that the complete illustration and expansion of the suggestions I have been making would require a volume instead of a newspaper article ; and I can only hope that these views will find some further explanation as I proceed.

It is notorious that when the apostles went abroad through the Roman empire preaching the gospel

and gathering converts into churches, slavery—
that is, labor without wages, the bondage of the
laborer to the employer, labor performed under the
authority and power of a master—slavery involving
the master's property in the servant—was everywhere the ordinary form of service. If that system
of slavery, as a system recognized and regulated by
law, was in some respects less atrocious than the
system which exists in our southern States, it was in
other respects more so. It was at once less atrocious and more atrocious than the system with which
we have to do, because the power of the individual
master was more nearly absolute, the state not troub-
ling itself to prevent either kindness or cruelty on
his part. The master could emancipate his slaves
if he pleased, and society did not refuse to receive
them as freemen. Or, without emancipating them,
he could educate them to any extent to which either
kindness or avarice might prompt him; and, when
they were educated, he could turn their talents and
acquirements to account in almost any employment.
On the other hand, if he was disposed to be cruel,
there was no severity which he might not practice
towards those who, in the unpitying eye of Roman
law, were to him just what the captive is, by the
laws of savage war, to his Indian captor. The slave
was liable to any torture upon any caprice of suspi-
cion—liable to death in any form at his master's will,
without even the allegation of a crime. And as to
the numbers of the slaves, it is enough to remember
that the poor could sell their children or themselves
for bread—that kidnapped children and women, not
negroes only, but of every language and complexion,

if carried to any considerable distance, could be sold with almost certain impunity—that every swoop of the imperial eagles, every plundered city, every conquered province swelled the myriads of the enslaved—that no triumph moved in glittering pomp from the Campus Martius to the Capitol, which did not glut the market with fresh herds of captives.

How did the apostles, and the churches under their personal instruction, conduct in respect to such a structure of society? Did they demand directly, everywhere, in God's name, the immediate and universal abolition of slavery? Did they exclude the master from communion simply for being a master? Was the relation of a master to a bond-servant, without any consideration of the master's conduct in that relation, counted and treated as a crime? I answer, without the least hesitation, *No.* I have given some serious attention, at various times, to the arguments of those who try to answer, *Yes ;* but I must confess, that whatever ingenuity there may be in them, and whatever respect may be due to the good intentions of their authors, they produce no conviction on my mind. The evidence that there were both slaves and masters of slaves in the churches founded and directed by the apostles, cannot be got rid of without resorting to methods of interpretation which will get rid of anything. The violence put upon the sacred records by High Churchmen, or by Universalists, does not exceed the violence with which these men, to whom I would impute no lack of reverence toward the Word of God, torture the Scriptures into saying that which the anti-slavery theory requires them to say.

How then (many an anti-slavery reader will be ready to ask) do I avoid the conclusion that the Bible warrants and sanctions slavery? How?— Simply by the all-sufficient consideration that the Bible, not being given to the world as a book of politics, and not undertaking at all to reform the world by prescribing forms of government, or by rectifying those political and civil relations which constitute the structure of society, seeks only to reconcile men to God, illuminating them from on high, and inspiring them one by one with principles of righteousness and love, and leaves the whole matter of civil and social improvement to the common sense of men thus enlightened and renewed. The fact that the Bible does not contradict the vulgar astronomy of the ages in which it was written, is impotent if urged against the demonstrations of Newton and Laplace. The fact that Jesus of Nazareth drafted no declaration of independence for Judea, is impotent as an argument against the self-evident truths of the American Revolution. The fact that Paul held no conventions, and uttered no protests, against the political system under which, in his days, the world was groaning, is impotent to prove that the Roman empire was not a system of outrage against right, and its history a history of inexpiable robberies and slaughters. Even so the fact that Christ and his Apostles did nothing in the way of denunciation or direct interference to abolish the relation of master and slave, and to introduce the better system of free labor for wages in its stead, is equally impotent to prove that the enslaving of millions of human beings in these United States, and their conversion by law

9

into mere chattels, robbed—so far as the state can rob them—of every human right, is not an atrocity fouler than the wrongs of Pharaoh against Israel, and worthy to be—as it is—the scorn and indignation of the world.

If it is the slaveholder who asks me how I avoid the conclusion that the Bible warrants and sanctifies slavery, I return the question to him. I put the inquiry to Governor Hammond and his associates in the task of vindicating " the peculiar institutions" of the south—Do you believe that the Bible warrants and sanctions the slavery which exists in South Carolina? Does your belief in the Christian religion require you to believe that the system which constitutes one-half of your human population mere merchandise—chattels—things incapable of suffering any injustice—is right before God, and ought to escape all censure from the moral sense of Christendom? Why? This is the only answer—Slavery existed in the Roman empire ; the apostles admitted masters of slaves to communion in their churches ; therefore slavery was right then ; therefore slavery is right now, right in principle and right in the details? Do you *believe* this, Mr. Hammond ? Then you believe that the slavery which the Apostles saw everywhere was right, for in this argument your belief that the slavery which now exists at Charleston is right, is only an inference from the righteousness of the slavery which existed eighteen hundred years ago at Antioch and at Rome. You believe that Christianity gave its Divine authority to sanction a system by which all captives in war were slaves in the hands of the captors, and were sold after a vic-

tory like sheep in the market;—a system which enslaved not negroes only but men of every complexion ; not savages only but men of the most civilized
races—the Jew with all the glory of his history and
his hopes, the Greek with all the beauty of Apollo
in his face and form, as well as the painted Briton
or the fair-haired Saxon ; not the degraded only,
born and trained to drudgery, but the refined and
cultivated, artists, poets, men of letters, as well as
" field hands" and " house servants." You believe
that if Napoleon, when his armies were sweeping
Europe, had brought back with him to Paris from
each vanquished country, myriads of miserable captives to be sold as so much plunder, and among those
myriads high-born ladies prized for their delicate and graceful beauty, [nobles torn from their
ancestral halls to be footmen on the carriages, and
cup-bearers at the banquets of the victors, artists
from the academies, and scholars from the universi-
ties, as well as mechanics from the towns and laborers from the fields—*that* slavery would have had its
warrant from the precepts of the gospel of love.* To
bring the argument nearer home—you believe that
if, in the contingencies of another conflict with Great
Britain, your State should fall for a time into the
power of the enemy, and the prisoners hurried to
the ships from your cities and plantations, should be
transported to London and sold there as you sell

---

* This argument from the character of Roman slavery, and this particular illustration, are presented with great force (if I remember aright
what I read ten years ago) by Dr. Channing. I would have used his
language rather than my own, if his little work on slavery had been, at
the time of writing, within my reach.

negroes, your wives and daughters for seamstresses
and chambermaids and children's nurses, your judges
and senators for attorneys' clerks, your merchants
and bankers for book-keepers and household stew-
ards, your men of literature and science for private
tutors, and your sporting gentlemen for grooms and
dog-whippers—Christianity would warrant and sanction the sale, and would rivet the chains forever upon
the limbs of all your chivalry. No! you do *not* believe that the gospel of the Anointed One, who came
to preach glad tidings to the poor, deliverance to the
captive, and the opening of the prison doors to them
that are bound, is the warrant of negro slavery;
and you deceive none but yourselves when you
say so.

But do I mean to say that the apostles, on the
principle of not meddling with questions of a political nature, permitted men bearing the Christian
name to treat their fellow-men as chattels, buying
and selling them like cattle, and driving them like
cattle with the whip? Do I hold that the apostles,
and the churches under their teaching, recognized as
believers and members of the body of Christ, men
who arbitrarily and violently separated children from
parents and wives from husbands, or who in any
way disregarded the human rights of those whom
the structure of society had placed as slaves under
their control? No!—no!—a thousand times, *No!*
Every passage of the New Testament which shows
that there were slaves and masters in the churches
of that age, and that the Apostles did not undertake
to abolish the relation by authority, shows also that
in that relation the master was to commit none of

these acts of wickedness. If I had reason to think that what I am writing would find its way to the south, to any considerable extent, I would go into the particular examination of the passages referred to. But I am writing for readers who, I am sure, will not challenge me to the proof when I say that in the primitive churches there was no more distinction between the master and the slave, on account of that relation, than there is in one of our churches between the householder and his hired man, or between the master mechanic and his journeyman; that a master who should be convicted of treating his slaves, converted or unconverted, otherwise than as the law of God requires every man to treat his neighbor, would meet with prompt rebuke and censure; and that the question in regard to a master's government and usage of his servants would be, not what does the law of slavery permit him to do, but what does the law of love plainly require him to do.

This, then, I understand to have been the apostles' method of dealing with slavery. They summed up the ethics of Christianity in the law of love; but many particular applications of that law were left, as of course they must be, to the common sense of individuals. The man who, professing to believe in Christ and to be governed by Christian principles, showed in his conduct that he was governed supremely by selfish passions—whether the love of pleasure or the love of gain, the love of ease or the love of power—was disowned as not having the spirit of Christ. The rich man and the poor man, the master and the slave, were tried by the same rule. No sumptuary laws were prescribed to limit the ex-

re p

penditures of the rich ; no tithing or *per centum* was
levied on his income, in the name of charity, by rule ;
how he should spend, and how he should give, it
was for his discretion to determine ; but if his conduct in these respects was such as to demonstrate a
supremely selfish disposition, he was of course rejected. It was not prescribed to the poor what stand
they should take for the assertion of their political
rights, what employments they should follow, or
how many hours should be a day's work ; but if the
poor attempted to throw themselves upon the church
for support, and to live in idleness and as scandal-
mongers, under pretence of devotion and religious
zeal, the rule was, " He that will not work, neither
let him eat." The slave was not instructed nor
stimulated to run away and try his capacity of self-
government and self-support ; nor was he told that
the gospel was his master's warrant for oppressing
him ; but he was expected to act, even in his servitude, from Christian principles, glorifying God, and
if his conduct toward his master, or toward any other
person, betrayed the dominion of a selfish spirit,
Christ and the church had no part in him. So the
master was not required to begin his Christian profession by dissolving the relation between himself
and his slaves, renouncing his authority and tutel-
age over them, and placing them out of his government and protection—though that was practicable
under the Roman law ; but if, retaining them under
his power, he treated them as his cattle rather than
as his fellow-men, immortal and responsible like
himself, and like himself redeemed with the blood
of Christ—if they were to him the mere instruments

of his indolence, his luxury, or his gains—if he did
not consider his power over them as a trust rather
than a possession, committed to him, in the arrangements of Providence, for their present and eternal
welfare rather than for his worldly wealth—if his
conduct toward them indicated the ascendency of
selfishness over conscience and love—then for those
specific things, whatever they were, which were the
indications of an unchristian character, he was liable
to censure in the form of admonition and rebuke;
and when admonition and rebuke were ineffectual
upon him, he became to the brotherhood " as a
heathen man and a publican."

I give out no challenge. I have no expectation
of being drawn into a vindication of my suggestions
in these essays, against any unfavorable judgment.
But I am confident that this representation of what
the Apostolic Christianity had to do with slavery,
is that which accounts for all the phenomena of the
New Testament records on the subject, and is that
which neither the defenders of slavery on the one
hand, nor the asserters of the anti-slavery formula
on the other, can set aside. In this view of the New
Testament teachings, I think we have the key which,
if rightly used, will unlock the difficulties of the
subject. The example of the apostles is our safest
guide in the administration of church government
over the masters of slaves.

Not to be misunderstood in any quarter, is more
than I dare to hope for. Yet let me ask the impatient reader, ready to denounce me for daubing with
untempered mortar, not to be too impatient, but to
contain himself, if he can, till next week, and read
again.

SHALL WE FOLLOW THE APOSTLES IN THEIR ADMINISTRATION OF
CHURCH GOVERNMENT OR SHALL WE TRY TO DO BETTER?

It is plain to me that in some particulars the conduct of the apostles respecting slavery, is not an example for us. Our political position, as citizens,
authorizes us to act as the apostles did not act, and
as they could not act consistently with common
sense. They, as subjects of the Roman government,
had no political power or responsibility ; and they
acted accordingly. If we were situated as they were,
it would be wise to do as they did. But we call ourselves freemen, in a free country. We may demand
of our fellow-citizens, whose equals we are, and with
whom we share in the sovereign power of the State
in which we reside, such measures, within the legitimate power of the State, as are suited to effect the
peaceful abolition of slavery at the earliest practicable date. We may demand of the government of
the United States, in which we have a voice as citizens of the Union, that in all its legislation, in all
its diplomacy, and in all its judicial and administra-
tive proceedings, so far as its legitimate powers extend, man shall be recognized as man, without regard to his complexion. We may demand that
where the jurisdiction of the United States is absolute and " exclusive," as in the District of Columbia,
and in territories not yet organized with legislative
bodies of their own, all those laws which constitute
the system of slavery, and by the force of which a

portion of the population are made mere chattels in
the possession of irresponsible masters, shall be swept
away. We may demand that the custom-house
shall recognize no human being as a piece of merchandise, and that no slave, as such, shall be entered
upon the manifest of a ship's cargo. We may demand that all slaves passing forth, upon the high
seas, with their masters' consent, beyond the jurisdiction of the local laws that make them slaves, shall
be free by the laws of the Union, as they are free by
the law of nations. And in a country like ours,
where thought and speech are free, where everything may be brought to the ordeal of discussion,
and where the deliberately formed opinions of the
people, as shaped by free inquiry and debate, are
sure to control, in time, the course of legislation and
of government, we may address ourselves to the
public in behalf of such an object, singly or in association, through the press or in the popular assembly, or in any way in which we can obtain a favorable hearing. We, as American citizens in this nine-
teenth century, have many things to do which the
apostles, in their age, and in their position as subjects of the despotism by which the world was governed, could not dream of doing.

But some will ask, Is not the conduct of the apostles, in this respect, an example for ministers of the
gospel, though not for men in other employments?
Undoubtedly, so far as ministers of the gospel are in
political relations like those in which the apostles
acted, they will do well to follow the example of the
apostles. If a minister of the gospel is called to perform
his ministry in a country where he is a mere subject,

9*

and not a citizen, and where he has no political rights
or functions, it will be best for him not to meddle
with political questions at all. But if he is a free
citizen of a republic, and as such shares in the responsibility of popular sovereignty, the example of
the apostles in abstaining from questions of legislation
and politics, is obviously no example for him. His
duty as a citizen, and how it is modified by his duty
as a minister of the gospel, he must ascertain for
himself, by the light of general principles, in the exercise of his own common sense.

It is not to be supposed that the apostles, in their
preaching, meddled at all with any political question,
or any point of legislation. We have no reason to
think that their oral discourses differed in this respect from their epistles. They required of masters,
not kindness merely, but—what is of far more sig-
nificancy—*justice*, toward their servants.* They
required of servants fidelity towards their masters.
But in respect to the abolition of slavery, and in respect to measures and arrangements tending towards
that end, they said nothing. Are we, therefore, who
are now ministers of the gospel in the United States,
bound to keep silence on the subject of slavery, save
as we reiterate the teachings of the apostles on the
relative duties of masters and slaves? I think not.
We are American citizens; and our hearers are
American citizens. Not only do we stand in a different position from that in which the apostles stood,

---

* A man may be *kind*, as language is ordinarily used, toward his
dog, or his horse ; he can be *just* only toward his fellow-men ; for *justice* implies *rights*.

but our hearers live, as it were, in another universe from that in which the hearers of the apostles lived. Our hearers are men to whom is entrusted the welfare of their country, and all coming generations; their moral and intellectual character as affected by the ministration of the Word of God, is one element of the power that controls laws and institutions, and determines all questions of public policy. So far as political questions are at the same time moral—questions of right and wrong, questions of the application of the law of love—so far it will be impossible for a free and faithful minister of Christ, rightly dividing the word of truth, entirely to avoid them. To keep such a question as that of slavery out of the pulpit, in such a country as this, must be impossible, as long as the pulpit is faithful to its trust in quickening the moral sensibilities, and in forming and guiding the moral judgments of those who sit under its influence. In a country where the question of war and peace, in a given emergency, is to be determined by the voices of the citizens, if the pulpit does not breathe into the minds of those who sit under it a just Christian abhorrence of war as a means of settling international disputes, the pulpit virtually defiles itself with blood. So in a country of free speech and thought, where millions of human beings are converted by law into chattels, and are treated as having no human rights, if the pulpit never, in any way, leads the hearers of the gospel to feel that, as citizens partaking in the sovereignty of the republic, they have something to do for the reformation of such injustice, it is so far recreant to the ends for which it exists; it abandons a great moral question to be determined by the low influences of selfish partisan politics. The preaching is not worth much, which does not help men to understand and feel what God would have them do in all their moral relations.

It is not necessary for me here to remark the limitations which a sound discretion imposes on the discussion of such questions in the pulpit. The man who has not common sense enough to avoid, in the pulpit, the agitation of certain questions of mere policy, which the legitimate application of the law of love leaves undetermined—still more the man who has not common sense enough to avoid questions merely personal, such as the merit or demerit of particular candidates for office—the man who makes his pulpit a place for repeating on the Lord's day, the substance of what he has been reading through the week in a partisan newspaper—the man who has a political hobby-horse which he rides in every sermon—will hardly learn much from anything that I can say to set him right. What I am insisting upon is not that ministers shall make themselves leaders in the strifes of political partisanship —not that the people shall go to church on Sunday to learn which ticket they must vote on Monday— but only that the absolute silence of the primitive preachers of the gospel, respecting the legislation and policy of the Roman empire, imposes no obligation on their successors in the United States, at the present day, to maintain the same silence respecting the legislation and policy of this country. We are not bound to follow even the apostles, blindly, but only as we see the principles on which they acted, and the application of those principles to our duties, in our relations. Christianity is not a religion of forms, or of merely specific regulations, but a religion of affections and of principles.

How is it, then, in regard to the administration of church discipline? Is the example of the apostles, in this respect, obligatory upon us? I answer, The *principles* upon which the apostles, and the churches under their personal direction, acted in respect to the admission and exclusion of individuals asking to be recognized as Christians, are principles which we cannot refuse to follow without rejecting the authority of the apostles. What are those principles? And in particular, what are the principles on which they acted in respect to the admission of masters and slaves to membership in the church? If they acted upon the principle that the mere relation of a master to his slaves, without considering his conduct in that relation, is irreconcilable with a Christian profession, and is therefore to be renounced " at all hazards ;" then we must adopt that principle and act accordingly, or else we must deny their authority. If, on the other hand, they evidently rejected that principle—if they recognize masters of slaves as believers—if when insisting on the duties of a master toward his slaves they never insist on an immediate legal emancipation—then it is quite plain to me that the master of a slave, simply for being such, if that is all that can be alleged against him, ought not to be excluded from communion in our churches, unless we can do better than the apostles did.

Can we, then, do better than they did? Setting aside their example, as not binding us to do likewise

—admitting that, through ignorance or inadvertence, or under the pressure of peculiar circumstances, the apostles and the churches under their personal direction may possibly have done that, in relation to slavery, which we ought not to do—let us inquire for ourselves, whether there is any sufficient reason, on what we recognize as Christian principles, for excommunicating every master of slaves, simply because he is a master.

At the risk of becoming wearisome by so much iteration, I must once more ask the reader not to misunderstand me, for I have the best reason to know that there are readers who have not yet apprehended the palpable distinction upon which I am insisting in all these articles. My doctrine is, that if the master of slaves refuses to recognize those slaves as his brethren of the human family—if he regards them and treats them not as his fellow men, for whose welfare he is in God's providence responsible, but as his property merely, his chattels, which he has a right to use as he pleases—if he does not use his power over them conscientiously, as a trust committed to him for their good—he is to be rejected by the church, because he does not deal with his servants according to the spirit of the law of love, and the positive precepts of the New Testament. That my doctrine is sound, so far as it goes; that the church has a right—nay, that it is bound to act upon my doctrine—is not in dispute. The question is whether the church has a right to go farther, and to demand of the master, under pain of excommunication, that he shall " at all hazards " dissolve the connection between himself and his slaves, shall divest himself of all power to govern or protect them, and shall leave them wholly and immediately to their own capacity of self-control, and to the tender mercies of a State that regards them as barbarians and as enemies.

On this question, I hold the negative; and the Anti-Slavery Society, as popularly and naturally understood, holds the affirmative. To put the question, and the reasons why I hold the negative, in a clear light, I will state not an extreme case, nor an imaginary one, but an actual instance of slaveholding. I have in my mind's eye a slaveholder whom, as I understand his character, no church has any right to exclude from its communion. There are obvious reasons why it should be improper for me to name him, or identify him before the public in any such way as would make him a subject of discussion in this part of the country or of jealousy among his neighbors. I know that such slaveholders as he are rare; but I would hope that there are more than one; and I trust that no individual will be designated, either here or at the south, as the only man between the Potomac and the Gulf of Mexico to whom my description can be applied.

The gentleman whom I have in view found himself, on coming of age, the lord of a plantation, and the master of (we will say) a hundred slaves. The plantation was his birth-place and the scene of his childhood; but he had been absent many years, as is often the case with southern young men sent to the north for an education; and at the age of twenty-one he returned to his home to take the control of his property, with a mind enlarged by liberal studies, and with a heart quickened, I doubt not, by the grace of God. Though a hereditary slaveholder, he inherited from his parents no passion for the vindication and maintenance of slavery; and his education in classical literature, his familiarity with history and with the lessons of political and moral science, his intercourse with liberal and enlightened men, and his personal observation of the effects of freedom upon the industry, intelligence and morals of the people, had inspired him with an intelligent and determined dislike of the system with which his birth had connected him. His mother and sisters had their rights in the estate when it came into his possession, but there was nothing in their views that was likely to embarrass him in any desire or attempt to do justice to the slaves.

Great was the joy of the negroes at seeing their own master among them; for they trusted that they were no longer to be under the control of administrators, or agents, or "hirelings whose own the sheep are not." Many were the greetings of old women who had borne him in their arms when he was an infant or had fanned him as he slept in his cradle—of old men who had been the confidential servants of his father long before "young master" was born, and of young men with whom he had played when they were little children together. But to him it was a day of sad and serious thought. What would God have him to do?—was the question. Had it been in his power to convert those slaves into a free peasantry, he would have done so, but *that* it was impossible for him to do. The State, in all the power which it had given him over those people, had given him no power to confer such a blessing upon them. What, then, was he to do? He had deliberated in his thoughts on the plan of removing them to some northern State, or to Africa, that there they might be free. But, while he felt that in that way he could soon rid himself of a painful care and burthen, and while he knew that the sale of his lands without the slaves would enable him to live in easy circumstances at the north; he was not convinced that the welfare of the slaves, or the welfare of the country, would be promoted on the whole, by such an arrangement. His conscientious conclusion was that the law of love—duty to those slaves—duty to his neighbors and their slaves—duty to his native State and to his country at large—required him to accept the trust which in the providence of God had been devolved upon him, and to fulfill that trust to the best of his ability. Accordingly he remains a slaveholder to this day.

I have been upon that man's plantation, and have had various means and opportunities of becoming acquainted with the system on which he is acting, and with his views in pursuing that system. It might not be right for me, without his consent, to attempt a description of the system in its details; and indeed my memory, unaided by any written document, might not be sufficiently exact for that purpose. A mere outline of the principles by which he is guided in performing what he regards as his duty will be sufficient. The idea which lies at the basis of his conduct in respect to his slaves, is not the idea that they are his chattels, and that he may use them as a northern farmer uses his oxen, for his own ends without any regard for their welfare; it is the contrary idea that they are his fellow-men, dependent on him for all that protection and control which a good government ought to exert over subjects so weak and helpless as they are. If the State would have permitted him to pay them wages for their work, and then to require them to provide their own supplies, I have no doubt he would have done so long ago. But not being able to do what he would he did the best that he could. Each family on his plantation has its house, with a certain amount of suitable furniture; its little plot of ground to be cultivated by the members of the family for their own pleasure or profit; its regular supplies of provisions, according to the number of the family; its new suits of clothing, at stated intervals, for man, woman and child; and its medicines and medical aid in sickness. In lieu of all that the free operative would pay for these accommodations out of his wages; and in lieu of all militia service, and all town, county and State taxes, each slave—for to them the master stands in the place not only of landlord and employer, but of town, county and State government—performs a certain daily task amounting to something more than half a day's labor. The remainder of the day they employ at their own discretion in their gardens or their houses, or in a field which the men are permitted and encouraged to cultivate in common on the plan of a joint stock company. The products of all this portion of their labor are their own—their *peculium;* and when they have anything to sell of their own raising, they have their choice to sell it to their master, if he wants it, or to send it to a neighboring market town. Their money, thus acquired, they expend for what they value as luxuries or comforts, or they hoard it for some future use they know not what. Their master told me that if in any emergency he should want to borrow a thousand dollars, and should be sure of being able to repay it speedily, he had no doubt he could raise that amount upon his personal credit among his slaves.

All the arrangements which I have mentioned were made, not in mere good nature towards the slaves, nor simply as the most economical system of management, but as part of a system of measures and influences for their improvement. There was much pains-taking by their master and by the ladies of the family, to inspire the people with the tastes and wants of civilization. There was a school for the children, where they had been taught to read, till some alarm in the country had compelled the teachers to confine themselves to other methods of instruction. Every evening, at a stated hour, the people of the little village were assembled in a room which served as chapel, where their master read the Scriptures to them and led them in worship. Once every week, besides the Sabbath services in which the whites and blacks of several plantations were united, the pastor of the church in the neighborhood preached to my friend's people in a style suited to their capacity; and they were even then beginning to like his preaching better than the noisy rant they had been used to, because it was instructive, or because in their phrase, they *could get hold of it better*. Their labor was stimulated, as I have shown, not by the slavish incitement of fear, but by the manlike impulses of hope and gain. The obedience required of them was felt to be obedience to salutary laws rather than to despotic will. Punishment, of whatever kind or degree, was inflicted, not as the master's wrath because his interests were neglected, but as the execution of law against what the conscience recognized as crime. Nor were crimes punished without the formality of a trial. And to develop and strengthen the sentiment of justice among the slaves some rudiments of trial by jury had been introduced into the administration of government over them.

Enough has been said, perhaps, for my purpose, but I want the whole case fairly stated. It is to be acknowledged, then, that the people on my friend's plantation do not consider themselves free; they are not free, they are slaves. The discipline on his plantation is not lax, but strict; his people are in every respect orderly, and are obliged to be so. It is to be acknowledged, also, that he makes money out of the labor of his slaves—more than most masters make on the same soil, who treat their slaves like cattle—though much less, I doubt not, than the China merchants of New York make out of the labor of their seamen, and less than the manufacturers on the Naugatuc make out of the labor of their well-paid operatives, and less than he might make if he should sell them all, and invest the proceeds in stock of the proposed railway between New York and New Haven. If it be asked whether he communes with his servants at the Lord's table, I am compelled to confess that he does not, for the reason that he is a Presbyterian, and they being Baptists, will not admit him to communion.

Here, then, is a slaveholder—a voluntary slaveholder—one, who in the exercise of his free agency,
accepts and sustains "the relation of master to those
whom the law makes slaves;" and the question is,
Shall he be cut off from the church simply because
he stands in this relation?

It may be argued that this man's policy is altogether mistaken—that by the kindness and justice
of his administration, as a master, he is doing nothing
for the anti-slavery cause, but is enabling such men
as I am to 'apologize for slavery'—that if he would
embrace the doctrine of immediate emancipation,
and make his slaves free by a formal act at all hazards, or if he would remove them to the north or
west, and make them free in a land of strangers, he
would do much more good than he is now doing—
that if he were to treat his slaves with the utmost
cruelty, starving them into skeletons, scourging them
to laceration, washing their stripes with aqua-fortis,
hunting them out of their refuges with bloodhounds,
he would be actually doing more than he is now
doing to hasten the downfall of the system. I will
not go into that argument, for it is not at all to the
purpose. Admitting that the man errs in judgment,
you cannot prove that he errs guiltily. Whether he
is wise or unwise, he is, beyond dispute a believer in
Christ; he takes the Holy Scriptures for his rule of
faith and practice; the law of love is written on his
heart by the spirit of God: whatsoever he would
that men should do to him, he is doing even so to
them. He has found these black "neighbors" who
long ago, on the highways of this wicked and plun-
dering world, had fallen among thieves, and had suf-

fered divers grievous wrongs, and had been left more than half dead; he is treating them with compassion, binding up their wounds, and pouring in oil and wine; he is putting them upon his own beast, and taking them to the inn. You may denounce him as a Samaritan because he rejects your formula; you may say that his treatment is not judicious, that his surgery is old-fashioned, and will never result in a cure; that he ought to use your patent nostrums, your hydropathic bandages, your homeopathic powders, your 'magical pain extractor,' and that if you had the patients in hand, you would cure them all in half an hour. All this may be as you say, I will not dispute it; but after all the man is a good Samaritan; he is neighbor to the poor negroes that had fallen among thieves; and there is neither principle nor rule, in the New Testament, which authorizes any church to exclude him from communion.

I need not deny that the cause of human liberty and of human happiness—the great cause of God in the world—would be more promoted, if the man of whom I am speaking should follow the example of a friend of his in the same county, who has removed his slaves to a free State, and has discharged himself of all further responsibility in respect to them. But is this so plain and certain, so infallibly revealed, that the man who does not see it may be censured by the church, and excommunicated for not seeing it? Who has not known many an instance in which a patient, who might have recovered with competent medical attendance, has died before his time, because his friends had more confidence in some advertising quack than in a scientific and skillful physician? Yet the church does not excommunicate such persons. Why not? Because, plain as the matter is to others, it is not plain to them; and it is not the province of the church to settle such questions. The friends who called in the quack were honest in so doing; they did it in pure love for the sufferer; they did it, praying for God's blessing; and though life was sacrificed, the church does not interpose with its censures. Questions of medical practice are not to be decided by the clergy, or by a church meeting. The Bible does not reveal God's will upon that subject. Clear as it may be to some of us that the policy which the man of whom I speak has adopted is erroneous, there is no infallible judge this side of Rome, to decide the question against his conscientious judgment.

I say, then, charge upon the slaveholder some specific crime, and prove it. Show that he treats his servants as mere property; show that he does not respect or guard their domestic relations; show that the chastity of their wives and daughters is not protected under his government; show that he keeps them in ignorance of God and of God's Word; show that he permits them to steal, to quarrel, to break the Sabbath, so that they do not injure him; show even that he runs in debt on the credit of what they would sell for if seized by the sheriff; and for any such thing he may be admonished by the church, and if he will not hear the church he may be excommunicated. But where has Christ given the church authority to decide upon forms of government, to proscribe political institutions, to adjust the relations between rulers and subjects?

NO. VI.

CHRISTIANITY AND THE CHURCH COUNTERACTING SLAVERY. HOW?

Suppose the gospel to be preached for the first time in a civilized slave state—civilized in the same degree in which the slave States of this Union are civilized—civilization being carried as far as is compatible with a structure of society so essentially barbarous. Suppose that the gospel, as a revelation of God's character and moral government, of the way in which sinners may be forgiven and saved, and of those divine truths by the spiritual perception of which the soul is renewed to holiness—is preached without any particular exposition of its bearings on the political institution of slavery, or even on the relative duties of masters and slaves. On the one hand, the consciences of the people have not been sophisticated with atrocious arguments in defence of slavery; on the other hand, the intrinsic injustice of the institution and the mischiefs which it works upon the morals, the intelligence and the industry of the community, have never been pointed out to them. To that people the gospel is preached in its principles—"repentance toward God and faith toward our Lord Jesus Christ." The all-comprehending law, "Thou shalt love the Lord thy God with all thy heart, and thou shalt love thy neighbor as thyself," is clearly announced as God's law for the universe. The character of God, who "hath made of one blood all nations of men," and who "now commands all men everywhere to repent, because he hath appointed a day in which he will judge the world in righteousness "—is exhibited in all the illustrations of its glory, which the gospel affords. Christ is " set forth evidently crucified," as " a propitiation for the sins of the whole world." It is proclaimed that " if any man be in Christ, he is a new creature," and that in Christ—in the bonds of allegiance and love to him, in the unity of communion with him— all the distinctions which divide men, whether distinctions of race or language, of nation or condition, are merged, and all are on one footing. These principles, we will suppose, find audience; and, by the grace of God, they enter into some hearts with a quickening power. How will they operate in respect to slavery?

The first effect of Christian principle on the mind of a master toward his slaves, is to make him recognize those slaves as his brethren of the human race, who, though they may not be his equals in the eye of the state, are his equals at the tribunal of God. Not only is that natural instinct strengthened and elevated, which prompts him to treat his servants kindly, as he would his dogs or his cattle, because they are his; but he is made to feel that these servants, placed under his power and protection, are, like himself, the subjects of God's government, rational and responsible; that like him they are made for immortality; that like him, involved in the ruin of a common apostacy from God, they are the objects of God's care and compassion, and of the redeeming love of One who gave himself a ransom for all. He feels that in the sight of God he and the meanest of his slaves are equal—equally worthless as sinful creatures, equally precious as immortal

10

souls. He feels, within, the movement of the Spirit of God's love, writing upon his heart and breathing into his soul's life the law, "Thou shalt love thy neighbor as thyself." The first impulse upon his mind is that these poor people are his neighbors, and must be treated accordingly; that he must do them good to the extent of his opportunities; that he must by all means make them acquainted with God and with the way of salvation; that the first of all his duties to his fellow-men, is his duty to these wronged and helpless creatures whose entire destiny, from this time onward, is so much within his power. Can he any longer treat these persons as things which, having no rights, can suffer no injustice? Can he treat them as merchandise, property, creatures made to be bought and sold? Can he leave them in the power of a mere hireling, a low and brutal overseer? Can he refuse to acknowledge and protect the domestic relations and affections which nature, too strong to be entirely subverted by oppression, has established among them? Must he not begin to treat them in all respects as men having the common rights of human nature? Must he not begin to treat them in all respects as men made in God's image, and redeemed from the wrath to come by Christ's atoning sacrifice? I am not speaking of how a man may act, who has received Christianity as a dead tradition including a divine warrant for enslaving the "cursed race of Ham." I am not speaking of how a man may act who knows the gospel only under the forms of a "hard-shell" Antinomianism. I am not speaking of what a Christian man may do contrary to the principle of Christian love, through inadvertence or under the power of some special temptation. I only ask the reader to imagine for himself the spontaneous operation of the " new heart and new spirit " in a master of slaves ; and I say that to him thus renewed by the gospel, those slaves are no more *things*, inferior creatures, whom he may use for his own pleasure or gain without any regard to their welfare, but fellow-men who are of as much worth in the sight of God as he is, and whose welfare he is bound by God's law to value as if it were his own.

Let us now extend our view somewhat. Instead of a solitary master receiving the gospel and acting under its impulses, without any aid or sympathy from other minds around him, we have—let us say —a dozen families living in habits of frequent amicable intercourse. Into each of these families, dispersed to some extent among families of a very different character, the gospel has entered with something of its renewing power. These families constitute a Christian congregation. The heads of these families, sustaining similar relations to the enslaved peasantry on their several plantations, as well as to their several household circles, are under each other's influence ; and as fellow-believers, they are watching over each other " to incite to love and good works." In their conferences and consultations, their duties in the various relations of life come into discussion, and are made the subject matter of mutua exhortation, and among the rest, not last nor least, their duties as masters, individually and collectively. As Christian men, moved by the spirit of Christ, they talk with each other about those slaves

of theirs, what shall be done for them; and in all
their debates the slaves, instead of being regarded,
according to the theory of the laws, as inferior creatures, beings without rights, mere property to be used
for the benefit of their owners, are regarded as men
whom God made in his own image, for his own service, and for immortal blessedness, and whom Christ
has redeemed. And in this way, the influence
which the gospel has on each individual apart, to
make him feel that the slave is his brother and must
be treated accordingly, and to make him ask, " He
that loveth not his brother whom he hath seen, how
can he love God whom he hath not seen?" is
strengthened by the association and Christian sympathies of the individuals with each other. Thus
we begin to see some rudiments of the legitimate
action of Christianity and the church against slavery. Christianity and the church recognize the
slave as a man, an immortal spirit, a creature having rights, his master's equal before God.

And as Christianity and the church extend themselves, slaves too begin to experience the quickening
power of the gospel. Here we have a new element.
In the church, the slave is not only a brother by the
tie of a common humanity, but a brother in Christ.
The master and the servant share in thoughts and
emotions, in experiences of infirmity and deliverance,
in joys and hopes, which place them on one level.
Both walking in faith and love, and breathing the
same spirit of adoption, both are alike the servants
of Christ and the freemen of the Lord. Consequently a new feeling of respect and affection springs up
in the mind of that master toward that servant. Nor

is this all. As religious instruction is communicated
to the slaves upon one plantation and another, and
as the fashion of teaching slaves the truths and duties
of Christianity spreads in the community, not only
is there an effect upon those who experience the full
power of the truth, but others partake in the movement. The servants of Christian masters first, and
then to some extent the enslaved as a class, rise
gradually, but steadily, in the scale of intellectual
and moral being. And as they rise; as they become more intelligent, more cultivated, more civilized; as their higher human nature, in distinction
from their merely animal instincts, is developed;
their brotherhood in the human family is more distinctly felt on all sides, and demands a more formal
recognition. While this process of reformation in
the ideas and sentiments of the people is going forward, the moment is steadily approaching in which
the laws will chronicle the change, and will acknowledge the slave as a *man*, for whose welfare the State
is bound to provide, and whose inalienable human
rights the State is bound to protect. Whenever that
moment arrives, a new order of things—which had
been preparing itself as silently perhaps, and perhaps as unsuspectedly, as some great process of cre-
ative nature—makes its appearance. The motion
on the dial-plate was slow—nay, imperceptible to
hasty and impatient eyes; but meanwhile the unrest-
ing pendulum within, and the weights and wheels,
were doing their office unobserved. At last the clock
strikes twelve; midnight is past, and though darkness still lingers, the hours of a new day begin to be
numbered.

But such a result will not be attained, or at least will be indefinitely postponed, unless Christianity is dispensed and exhibited in the form of church discipline. A lax administration of church discipline, in respect to the conduct of masters towards their servants, will accomplish, more speedily and effectually than can be done in any other way, the complete degradation of Christianity, and will especially and primarily counteract its legitimate operation against slavery. Let us observe, then, how church discipline will be administered in a slave State like that presented in our hypothesis—a state in which the gospel has begun to be preached without any pro-slavery or anti-slavery commentary, and in which there have begun to be believers, both masters and servants, who have received the gospel, not as a tradition of dogmas and regulations, but as life in Christ and in the Spirit of God. The answer, I think, cannot be difficult to any man who understands what effect the gospel produces on a mind regenerated by its power. All will agree with me in affirming that the administration of church discipline, in the circumstances represented by our hypothesis, will include the following particulars.

1. Members of the church, if they are masters of servants whom the law regards as property only, and whom the law therefore treats as having no personal rights, will not be allowed by the church to regard their servants as the law regards them, or to treat them as the law treats them. The master who buys or sells his fellow-men for gain, or out of regard to his own convenience merely, will be admonished, and if he does not repent will be excommunicated;

and the consideration that the law permits him to do so will no more be admitted as a justification, than the parallel fact that the law of New York refuses to recognize fornication or adultery as a crime, would be admitted as a reason why the church may not censure those who are guilty of such offences. The master who disposes of his servants just as he would dispose of any other property—giving them away, hiring them out, or otherwise using them simply for his own ends, without regard to their wishes and interests—will be admonished like any other offender, and if admonition is ineffectual, will be excluded from the communion of the saints. The master who, because the law regards slaves as incapable of acquiring or possessing property, will not allow his servants to have anything which under his protection and government they can call their own, who permits them to have no time that is theirs, no earnings or savings that are theirs, and who treats them in no other way than as a humane man treats his cattle, will be dealt with by the church as one who gives no evidence of being actuated by the spirit of Christ.

2. The relation of master to servant, where servants are slaves, is one which involves constant temptation to acts of passion and of injustice in the administration of power. For all such acts a master who professes to be a believer is accountable to the church. The master of a ship at sea is intrusted, necessarily, with a despotic power over the sailors. All men know how liable that power is to be misemployed, how many acts of cruelty are perpetrated on shipboard, in passion or caprice, or by the

deliberate abuses of the power committed to the master. All men know, too, that if a shipmaster is a member of a church, and there comes to that church the report of any such offence on his part, the matter will surely be investigated, and the offence, if proved, will be visited with appropriate censure. Just so in a church which contains masters of slaves, and in which Christianity has not become a tradition corrupted by the expositions of such rabbis as Gov. Hammond, every instance of passion or injustice in the administration of the master's government, will be the subject-matter of church censure. The church will no more permit cruel or unjust punishments to be inflicted on slaves whose master is responsible to the church for whatever concerns his Christian character, than it would permit a passionate and cruel master to inflict the same punishments on hired servants or apprentices.

3. The church which goes to this extent in watching over such members as sustain the relation of which we were speaking—and to this extent it must go if it does not utterly dishonor the name of Christ —will necessarily go farther. There are some obvious positive duties, which a master in fellowship with the church cannot be permitted to neglect. It is not enough for him to abstain from direct personal acts of cruelty and oppression; the slaves have a right to look to him for the blessings of good government and protection, so far as it is in his power to dispense such blessings; they have a right to look to him, for they can look nowhere else. The first of all their rights as human beings living in society, a right which transcends even their right to personal liberty,

is their right to be governed, and well governed, and to have all that protection from their own evil propensities, and from the evil propensities of other men, which good government affords. He can hardly be guilty of a greater wrong against them, than that which he commits, if through any neglect of his, they are not protected as men and governed as men. If, then, he fails to place them under such a system of regulations as is suited to promote their individual and social well-being—if he does not care for and protect their persons, their little possessions and their morals—if he neglects to guard, as a magistrate, the chastity of females, or to uphold the sanctity and permanence of the marriage tie—if he neglects to restrain them from petty larcenies against each other, and from quarrels and fightings—if he allows or connives at drunkenness and rumselling among them—if he does not require them to keep the Sabbath by resting from unsuitable occupations—his brethren in the church will not fail to admonish him, and when admonition has been found ineffectual, they will disown him.

4. Nor will this be all. The relation which he sustains to his servants, as being to them in the place of the State, involves only a part of his positive duties towards them. As a Christian man looking upon the ignorance and debasement of these his dependent neighbors, he is bound to care for their entire welfare as spiritual and immortal beings. He is bound—and by all the movements of the Spirit of Christ within him he is impelled—to provide instruction for them, and especially to make them acquainted with God and with the way of salvation

10*

through Christ. If he neglects this duty, if his servants are permitted to live and die in heathenish ignorance, if he does not labor in the spirit of self-denying love to win them to God, and to train them for God's service and for immortal blessedness, the church will strive to bring him to a sense of his duty, and finding him incorrigible, will declare that he has not the spirit of Christ and is none of his.

Such being the administration of church discipline in the community which we have supposed, it is evident that there the slaves of " believing masters" will be treated, and their masters will be required by the church to treat them, in effect, as if they were hired servants, or apprentices, under the protection of law. How obvious is it that such an administration of Christianity will tell, gradually perhaps, but infallibly, on the entire character of that community, quickening and guiding the moral sense of the whole people. How obvious that in that community the human sentiment which recognizes the slave as a man, and which acknowledges his human rights— the sentiment which when it comes to assert itself through the forms of legislation, will speedily work out the abolition of slavery—cannot but be making progress. How obvious that in that community not only the slaves of " believing masters," but the whole of the enslaved population, will be continually and irresistibly rising in their intellectual and moral character, and commanding more and more of the respect of the ruling class. How obvious that Christianity, thus administered, will spread itself in that community, and will act with a power continually increasing, till every fetter is broken, and the soil, no longer exhausted by the curse of slavery, shall brighten into beauty like Eden, and shall give up its riches freely, to fill the hands of free and happy industry. Where Christianity is clearly and faithfully preached as the law of the spirit of life in Jesus Christ, and where it is administered in the form of a legitimate and fraternal church discipline, slavery must be a transient institution, for slavery belongs entirely to that order of things which the ascendency of Christianity annihilates. Christianity civilizes, all its tendencies are towards the highest possible forms of social order and improvement: slavery is essentially barbarous. Christianity humanizes, it develops the faculties and affections of true manhood in every individual whom it reaches: slavery brutalizes. The genius of Christianity is love and good will: the genius of slavery is violence and fear. Christianity makes all men equal in God's regard, equal before the dread bar of justice, equal at the cross, equal at the throne of grace, equal in the church: slavery abhors the idea that every man is, in respect to rights, the equal of his fellow-man; it rejects the law of thought which makes justice and *equity* (or equalness) convertible terms in every human language. Christianity is light, it quickens every mind into intelligence, it pours upon all souls an illumination from the skies: slavery is of the darkness, it hates and dreads the light, it seals up the souls of men in ignorance, it gathers around itself night deep and murky, for darkness is its element. Christianity and slavery, wherever they co-exist, must needs be like the Ormuzd and Ahriman of the Persian mythology—the opposite principles of light

and darkness—forever contending each to subdue the
other. If Christianity continues to hold forth its
light, in that light slavery must decay and perish.
If Christianity yields, obscures its light, and enters
into a confederacy with darkness, it decays and dies
in the chains of its captivity.

I dare not ask for another column in this week's
paper*; and therefore, though I am anxious to bring
the discussion to a close on my part, I must post-
pone the application which I intend to make of
these remarks, till I can have another hearing.
Meanwhile it will not have escaped the reader's
notice, that though I commenced with a review of
the action taken by the Board of Foreign Missions,
and though the general title with which I began has
been retained for the sake of marking the continuity
of the series, I have in view not merely the specific
missionary question touching the Cherokee and
Choctaw churches, but that more comprehensive
and momentous ecclesiastical question, with reference to which the debates at Brooklyn were con-
ducted. The time has come, when the ministers of
the gospel and the professed followers of Christ, individually and in their various ecclesiastical assemblies, are called to inquire calmly yet earnestly, whether the churches in the slaveholding States, with
which they are respectively in communion and correspondence, are really acting in conformity with
Christian principle towards such of their members as
are owners of slaves. The reports are such concerning the administration of discipline on this subject in
the southern churches—the extent to which those reports have gained belief throughout the Christian

world is such—that, in the absence of any authentic denial of their truth on the part of those churches, the question, *What ought we to do in this matter ?* must come up in all the ecclesiastical bodies with which those churches are in correspondence. It is well known what arrangements are in progress to urge this question effectually upon the notice of the Triennial Assembly of the Presbyterian Church, now soon to meet. It is equally well known that the same question will be introduced again—as it has been heretofore under one form and another—in those Congregational bodies of New England which are in correspondence with the two divisions of the Presbyterian Church. This question ought not to be evaded or postponed ; nor can it be much longer.

Those who have favored me with letters, anonymously or otherwise, proposing particular points for my consideration, will probably find their inquiries answered, either formally or informally, before I close. Every communication which in any way helps me to know how far I am understood or misunderstood, is thankfully accepted, though it may not be in my power to make any other than this general acknowledgment.

NO. VII.

DUTY OF THE CHURCHES IN THE FREE STATES.

THE idea of communion among Christian churches, or between confederacies of churches, implies some degree of responsibility in regard to the maintenance of church discipline. Much more is this implied, where communion takes the form of a settled correspondence and regulated intercourse. Such mutual responsibility, necessary as the basis of mutual recognition, is not inconsistent with mutual independence and mutual equality of powers. In the language of the Cambridge Platform, (ch. xv. §2,) illustrating this principle, "Paul had no authority over Peter, yet when he saw Peter not walking with a right foot, he publicly rebuked him before the church. Though churches have no more authority one over another than one Apostle had over another, yet as one Apostle might admonish another, so may one church admonish another, and yet without usurpation." I quote this not as "authority," but as good common sense well expressed.

I need not, then, spend any time in showing that the churches in the free States have a right to concern themselves with the manner in which discipline is administered, or not administered, in the Southern churches. The only questions are, whether there is in existing facts an occasion for the exercise of this right; and if so, in what form and by what procedure shall the right be exercised?

To the first of these questions, the existing facts are a sufficient answer. A "common fame" has spread through this land, and has been sounded out to the ends of the world, which charges upon the southern churches, indiscriminately, a scandalous neglect of Christian discipline. It is charged upon those churches that members in full communion, office-bearers, ministers, commit, uncensured, and habitually, crimes which cause the name of Christ to be blasphemed. It is charged upon them that communicants, elders, pastors, preachers of what pretends to be Christianity, are tolerated in treating their servants, whom barbarous laws have put into their power, as mere property, to be bought and sold for gain, or at the convenience or caprice of the buyer and seller. It is charged that masters in the communion of those churches are tolerated in governing their servants and dealing with them, not as human beings having human rights, but as cattle driven to their labor with the whip, moved by no human impulse to industry, and having no more interest in their own labor than the muzzled ox " that treadeth out the corn." It is charged that the servants of such masters live and die without the knowledge of God's illuminating and quickening Word ; with no advantages or means for the development of their nature as intelligent beings created in God's image; borne down under an oppression heavier, in this most vital respect, than that which degrades the subjects of Russian or Austrian despotism, more unchristian than even that which keeps down the slaves of Antichrist himself within the immediate civil jurisdiction of Rome. It is charged that servants of such masters, when their masters might protect them, are robbed of God's primeval institution of marriage; that instead of being permitted to live together, husband and wife, in a relation which can be dissolved only by death, or by crime on their part, they live, male and female, in a temporary pairing unsanctioned by religion, unprotected by power, and liable to be dissolved at the convenience of the master. It is charged that the chastity of female servants, under such masters, has no protection

against the frauds or the violence of licentiousness.
It is charged that by the authority of such masters,
children are torn from the fathers and mothers to
whom God gave them, and are sold as merchandise.
I do not make these charges against the southern
churches ; nor do I take it for granted that these
charges are all true. What I say is, that these charges
are uttered by " common fame "—are believed
by millions—are carried abroad to the farthest out-
posts of civilization in every quarter of the world—
have never been disproved—have never been met
by those churches with anything like an adequate
and authentic denial.

In the existence of such facts there is, beyond controversy, an imperative occasion for the exercise of
that right of inquiry and admonition on the part of
other churches, which is inseparable from the idea
of communion. If these charges, so widely published, and so widely believed, are not a sufficient
reason for putting the churches of the slaveholding
States upon their defence, nothing can be. The imputations against their Christianity are not less serious than if they were charged with tolerating in
their communion the rationalism of Germany, the
fooleries of Oxford, and the impostures of Rome and
of Nauvoo. In some way they should be summoned, as churches, to answer for themselves
whether these things are so. And if they refuse to
meet the inquiry, or fail to vindicate themselves ; or
if, admitting that the matters of fact alleged against
them are true, they do not repent under admonition,
then the communion between those churches and
the churches of the north and of the west must end.

The right of every northern ecclesiastical body to withdraw communion, in such a case, from the southern churches, would be too manifest to be questioned.

In what form, then, and by what course of procedure, may this right of inquiry and of ultimate non-communion be most advantageously exercised? On this point, it will be sufficient to advert to the established relations and formal correspondence between the southern churches of various denomina tions, and those churches in the free States with which they agree in the forms of doctrine and of worship.

The General Assembly of the Presbyterian church exercises, by the terms of its constitution, a general superintendence over all the affiliated synods, presbyteries and congregations. Every subordinate judicatory is responsible to the assembled representatives of the whole communion, for all its errors or deficiencies in respect to the administration of discipline, and is, accordingly, liable to be admonished or instructed by the General Assembly. Such being the fact, can there be any doubt as to what the General Assembly—whether Annual or Triennial —can do, and ought to do, in reference to the '*fama clamosa*' of which I have spoken ? Let the General Assembly take notice of this ' crying fame' which so dishonors, not only the Presbyterian church as a great confederacy of Christian congregations, but also the name of Christ himself ; and by that supreme judicatory let it be enjoined on all presbyteries and church sessions, to inquire whether any of the ministers or members under their care are guilty of the sins thus charged upon the Presbyterian

church, to visit such offenders with due censure
wherever they may be found, and to report hereafter, at each General Assembly, whether such
crimes are indeed tolerated or winked at within their
respective jurisdictions. It is in the power of each
synod in the free States, nay, of each presbytery or
church session, to address the General Assembly
with reference to so great a scandal, and to demand
some decisive action for the removal of the reproach.

The Congregational bodies in New England, and
in the other northern States, have no churches in
the slaveholding States, and therefore are not
directly implicated in these charges. Yet their
ecclesiastical intercourse with the Presbyterians of
the south is so intimate, that it could hardly be
more so if the two denominations were fused into
one. Church members and ministers pass from one
communion to the other continually, as easily as
they pass from one part of the country to another.
As far as New England is concerned, the various
Congregational organizations maintain communion
with each of the two great divisions of the Presbyterian church by an interchange of delegates. Thus
the Congregational body in each of these five States
has a stipulated right to speak to the General
Assembly in the same way in which one Congregational church, according to the Cambridge Platform, may speak to another. If then, at the
approaching sessions of the General Assembly, that
body—either of the two bodies bearing that name
—shall neglect to take some efficient measures for
the removal of the great scandal, which for some
twenty years has been continually growing, till it

has become offensive to the moral sense of Christendom, it will remain for the New England Congregational Associations and Conventions, at their
meetings immediately following, to take up the
subject, and separately or jointly to expostulate with
the General Assembly on its unchristian neglect of
Christian discipline. Then, if at the end of another
year such admonition shall not have been duly
noticed—if the scandal remains untouched by the
judicatory immediately responsible for it to the
Christian world—if the one Assembly shall have
been too much occupied with the scandal of young
people's dancing, to attend to such a scandal as this
—if the other Assembly shall have been so engrossed
with the question whether the Rev. Mr. McQueen
shall or shall not violate the law of North Carolina
by putting away his wife, that it can do nothing
towards refuting or removing the imputation which
makes it responsible for innumerable acts of oppression—it will be for these Congregational bodies to
take another step, and by a solemn act and declaration before the world, to dissolve all the existing
relations of intercourse and correspondence with the
General Assembly—which ever it may be—that has
proved recreant. From that time forward, the way
will be plain for every Congregational church in
New England, to withhold all acts of communion
from every southern church which does not distinctly clear itself from this scandal.

If, on the other hand, the General Assembly, or
rather the two Assemblies, should take decisive
measures in relation to the scandal of which I am
speaking—if orders should go down from Philadelphia

next May, requiring all the presbyteries and church sessions south of Pennsylvania to take notice of certain specifications alleged by common fame against their administration of church discipline, and enjoining upon them an immediate and un-shrinking attention to every instance in which a master does not render to his servants strictly, so far as his power over them extends, that which is just and equal—what would the result be in relation to those churches? Of course, it is impossible to foretell. The worst that could happen would be the immediate withdrawal of those presbyteries and congregations from all connection with the Presby-terian body. And if that event should come to pass, *from such a cause*, few would regret it; for such action on the part of those churches, in such circum-stances, would be an unqestionable demonstration that the common fame of which I have spoken is true—too true to bear investigation. And what branch, I will not say of the Presbyterian church, but of the universal church of Christ, is that which would desire to retain in its connection congregations so defiled with the guilt of inhuman oppression, and so obstinately and passionately resolved upon cleaving to that iniquity? My own belief is that this would not be the result; that in certain districts of the south, the churches would rejoice in such an opportunity of defending themselves against the imputations under which they suffer; that in those churches the administration of discipline would be greatly invigorated; that on the other hand, such churches as proved contumacious, would be dis-graced even in their own consciences and in the

eyes of oppressors around them, and if not utterly
abandoned to delusion and sin, would presently
begin to reform themselves ; and that the legitimate
living power of Christianity and the church to
counteract slavery, and to effect its abolition by
effecting a change in the sentiments and habits of
society, would soon begin to be manifested throughout the south.   In this way I should expect to see
the principle introduced into the southern churches
and gradually propagated there, that the holding of
a slave is *prima facie* evidence of wrong-doing, that
it creates some presumption of guilt on the part
of the master, and puts upon him the burthen of
showing that he is actually loving mercy, doing
justly, and walking humbly before God.   This
principle has been proposed and urged more than
once, with great power, by Dr. Robert J. Breckin-
ridge.   If he will carry this principle through, and
cause it to become law in the synod of his native
State, *sit mihi magnus Apollo.*   Thenceforth let all
that he has said and done against New England be
forgotten.

It remains to show what I regard as the advantages of this course of procedure, over that which is
commonly understood to be proposed by the Anti-
Slavery Society.   The proposal of the Anti-Slavery
Society, as language is ordinarily understood, is that
slaveholding itself—the simple relation of a master
to those whom the law of the State regards and treats
as slaves—shall be the subject matter of admonition,
and then, if not abandoned, of excommunication.
Our proposal, on the other hand, is that the exercise
of a despotic power, in any specific form of injustice

or oppression, shall be the subject matter of censure. Our proposal admits that, inasmuch as the possession of despotic power is ordinarily accompanied by some wrong-doing in the acquisition or in the use of it, it may be a reasonable rule of discipline to regard the mere possession of such a power as *prima facie* evidence of sin, and as constituting at least an occasion for investigation. The other proposal regards the power itself as sin, and excommunicates the master simply for standing in that relation.

The first advantage of our proposal is, that all who love justice and mercy, and really desire the abolition of slavery, can unite upon it. Men whose reverence for the Scriptures forbids them to adopt the anti-slavery formula, and who yet love righteousness and hate oppression, can act in this procedure. Nor do I see how any anti-slavery man can refuse to concur in it so far as it goes. He may find fault with it because it does not go far enough ; but how can he lift his voice or his hand to oppose it? He may hold his own distinctive principle uncompromised, and yet vote to enforce the discipline of the church against all those definite specific sins which are none the less sinful if his principle is true. But on the other hand, there are multitudes of men in the churches and in the ministry, this side of Maryland, who do not adopt, and cannot be made to adopt, the mode of discipline recommended by the Anti-Slavery Society. It is easy to denounce these men as actuated by the most unchristian motives, and to imagine that they can be coerced into conformity, but after all they are neither fools nor rogues. It is easy to say of them, as an anonymous "fellow-sinner" of mine, who writes to me from New York, says, in the fervor of his spirit, "Hell never enacted upon our miserable earth a species of wickedness too base to find clerical defenders and apologists. War, murder, inquisitions, drunkenness, despotism, and lastly, that sum of all villanies, slavery, have never wanted advocates among the clergy." But after all, the men of whom I speak are conscientious in standing off from the Anti-Slavery Society, and the men of the Anti-Slavery Society know it, even while denouncing them. Doubtless such men as Jeremiah Day, Noah Porter, Lyman Beecher, Leonard Woods and Moses Stuart, not to extend the catalogue, are as "grasshoppers," in the eyes of the Anti-Slavery Society; but after all, in any attempt to secure the application of church discipline to the masters of slaves, it is better to have even such men with you, if thereby you can do something without compromising any principle, than it would be to insist upon a course in which they cannot follow you.

Another advantage which our proposal has, is that it presents an issue upon which slaveholders cannot sophisticate their consciences as they do in their argument with the Anti-Slavery Society. 'Slavery, or slaveholding,' says the Society, 'is necessarily, and in all circumstances, the sin of the slaveholder, and therefore the slaveholder, if after admonition he does not renounce his authority, at all hazards, is to be excommunicated as an incorrigible sinner.' 'No!' says the slaveholder, 'the Bible is not written on this principle; in the Old Testament, and in the New, the Scriptures recognize servitude as an actually existing relation; nor did Christ or his apos-

tles enjoin on masters any duty of immediate eman-
pation, at all hazards, as a condition of salvation,
or as a condition of membership in the church.'
Having thus met the issue raised by the Anti-
Slavery Society, and having answered their position,
as it is easy for him to do to his own entire satisfaction, he feels that the Bible is on his side; if "the
Abolitionists" are wrong, he, of course, is right;
slavery is therefore all right, and he has nothing to
do in the case but to support himself by the labor of
his slaves if he can, or by selling them if their labor
proves too unproductive. But our proposal presents
another issue, and one which the slaveholder cannot get rid of so easily. It comes to him with the
question, What are you doing for those poor neighbors of yours, over whose welfare for time and for
eternity the providence of God has given you a
power so full of awful responsibility? How are you
treating them? Do you pretend that God has given
to you the dominion over them, as over the beasts of
the field? Do you treat them as if they were your
cattle? Or do you treat them as your fellow-men,
your equals before God, and according to the law,
Thou shalt love thy neighbor as thyself? Is their
toil for you, uncompensated toil? Or is the power
which you have over them so administered by you,
that the relation between you and them exists, in fact,
for their benefit, rather than for yours? If you rob
those helpless beings of their human rights—if you
do not render to them that which is just and equal—
your pretence to be a Christian is a foul dishonor to
the Christian name.

It is another advantage of our proposal that it is

the very thing which the Anti-Slavery Society professes to propose when it undertakes to define its
own position. Since I began the publication of these
articles, some one has sent me the Anti-Slavery Reporter for July, 1845, containing the official account
of the proceedings of the Society at its last annual
meeting. Among the twenty-three resolutions adopted on that occasion, to many of which I could most
heartily subscribe, the following is marked with a
pen for my special attention :

" 10. *Resolved,* that by slaveholding this Society understands
the holding and treating of human beings as property ; and main-
tains that to hold and treat a human being thus, is universally
and always sinful, and ought to be everywhere immediately
abandoned."

Let us take this, then, as an authentic exposition
of what the Anti-Slavery Society means when it
demands that the churches shall, by the proper
course of discipline, exclude all slaveholders from
their fellowship. " This sin," as they say in the
resolution immediately following—the sin thus defined—" the holding and TREATING of human beings
as property"—this, and not the sin of being a master of slaves, " is inconsistent with Christian character and a regular standing in the church of Christ,
and ought to be made the subject of remonstrance
and discipline, according to each one's distinctive
methods of procedure, in every branch of that
church." Need I say that this is just what I am insisting upon ? This identical sin of holding and
treating men as property is one of those sins connected with slavery, for which I would have discipline
administered in all the churches.

11

Where then do I differ from the Anti-Slavery Society? Just on this point. I utterly repudiate their definition of slaveholding. I deny that they have any right to make such definition. Their attempt to do so is a fraud upon themselves and upon the public. Such a definition is an abuse of words fit only to juggle with. It is the fountain-head of a perpetual stream of sophistry. Words have a meaning of their own which cannot be set aside by an arbitrary definition. Words, and especially such words as we have to do with in political and moral inquiries, are not like the arbitrary symbols of algebra which bear any meaning we choose to put upon them for the particular operation in which we are using them. I have no right to say that Trinity church spire is surmounted by a Turkish crescent, even though I explain myself by saying that crescent means cross.

My objection to the resolution which I have quoted, is that it is not true. It is not true as a definition; neither is it true as an averment of what " the Society understands by slaveholding." No doubt the gentlemen of the Society think they mean by slaveholding what the resolution says they mean. No doubt they think that by slaveholding they mean not only the holding of slaves but the holding of them *as property*, and the *treating* of them as property. No doubt they are perfectly unconscious of the transparency with which their cardinal sophism shines through the very language in which they wrap it up : ' Resolved, that by slaveholding we mean slave*holding* AND a certain kind of treatment.' This very series of resolutions shows that in spite

of their unanimous resolve, they do not mean what
they intend to mean. In the eighteenth resolution
they declare " that for missionary boards to appoint
and support slaveholders as missionaries is a violation of the spirit and teaching of Christ." What are
they talking about in this eighteenth resolution?
The very thing that they have been talking about
year after year in their continued assault upon the
American Board of Missions respecting the case of
the Rev. J. Leighton Wilson, lately of Cape Palmas
and now at the Gaboon. Mr. Wilson is or was the
master, the owner of certain slaves in Georgia, and
is therefore, or was, a slaveholder in the legitimate
meaning of the word; but to say of him that he
holds *and treats* those men as property is a calumny
for which I cannot believe that the authors of those
resolutions intended to be responsible. The fact is,
that by that word 'slaveholder' they understand just
what other people understand by it, 'the master of
a slave;' and then from their arbitrary definition of
slaveholding they derive the irresistible corollary
that every slaveholder holds his slaves as property
and treats them accordingly.

I have been for several years past not very familiar
with the current anti-slavery publications; but I
rarely light upon a newspaper of that class which
does not contain some specimen of this sophistry.
Thus in a number of the "Liberty Press," published
at Utica, (Jan. 18, 1846,) which has happened to
fall in my way, I find a communication commenting
on a paragraph from the "Dayspring," descriptive
of slavery and the slavetrade in Abyssinia. " The
gospel," says the Dayspring in that paragraph,

" seems to be the only sure means to put an end to these horrid customs." This sentence the writer in the Liberty Press takes for his text, and after premising that the Dayspring is published by the American Board of Foreign Missions, he gives out in an interrogative form the slander that this is "the same Board of Foreign Missions which, after solemn deliberation and discussion, resolved to employ slaveholders as their agents in foreign countries to propagate that gospel." I call this a *slander*, for it is not only not true in the false and forced sense which the Society in its definition tries to attach to the word ' slaveholding,' but it is not true in any sense. But let us go on with this writer. "It would be amusing," he says, "to hear one of these agents preaching, as Mr. Smith would say, gospel politics to the people of Abyssinia, whose overseer in Carolina was perhaps at that moment chaffering with a negro buyer about the price of a handsome female slave for the New Orleans market." See the sophism! If Mr. Wilson is, or was, a slaveholder, then by the very definition of slavery, he holds AND *treats* human beings *as property ;* and of course he sells the female slave, high-priced because of her beauty, for the New Orleans market. The writer adds, " There can be no doubt that a part of the funds of this Board of Foreign Missions consists of the avails of the sales of husbands, wives, parents and children, separately, to slaveholders in different and distinct parts of this extensive country." Of course there can be no doubt of it in the mind of a man who reasons in this way. Such calumnies thrown about " thick as leaves in Vallambrosa," are

the natural product of the primal sophism, ' slaveholding is slaveholding AND something more.' Such
a sophism assumed as a first principle, taken into
the soul and kept there till it affects the entire system,
becomes a disease of the intellect and of the moral
faculties, which shows itself in the passionate belief
and the reckless utterance of what any sane man
would know to be falsehood. When I see such
things, I cannot but be reminded of the language in
which the prophet sets forth the morbid effect of idol
worship on the intellectual and moral nature : "He
feedeth on ashes ; a deceived heart hath turned him
aside that he cannot deliver his soul nor say, Is there
not a lie in my right hand ?"

When I began this series of communications, I
had no expectation whatever of taxing to so great an
extent the patience of the editors and readers of this
journal. But having begun, I found myself constrained by a sense of duty to go on. Had I written
for the sake of writing, I should have written on
some other theme, on which I might write more
easily and with less hazard to my own good name.
My experience heretofore has shown me that when
I write on this subject, I must make up my mind to
encounter reproach from the most opposite quarters.
But I have not suffered this, or any other consideration personal to myself, to restrain me from speaking
what seems to me to be truth, important and timely.
I have not written with a view of confirming what
others have written whose views I presume to be
generally coincident with my own; for though I am
aware that Professor Pond has been writing in the
New England Puritan, and Dr. Edward Beecher in

the Boston Recorder, it has not been convenient for
me to read either their articles or what Mr. Phelps
has written in reply ; and as for Dr. Woods' two
communications in the Puritan, which I have read
with great pleasure, I knew nothing of them till
most of my articles were written. At what seems
to me a serious crisis in the history of our country
and of Christianity, I have written to express my
deep and long-matured convictions, and thus to discharge my own soul of the burthen which I felt that
God had laid upon me.

What I have to expect from the organs of the
anti-slavery party, it is not difficult to conjecture.
A question will be raised about my motives; or
rather my motives will be represented as unques-
tionably selfish and base.   Last autumn I had occasion, in reply to an assault from the south, to publish
a letter to the editor of the Philadelphia Observer,
which the readers of the Evangelist may remember.
That letter was copied into the Emancipator, with
something like a column of commentary in this
vein :*

" Some are trying to see how far they can carry their concessions in favor of slavery, without absolutely awakening public
indignation against themselves at the north.   Others are with
equal assiduity trying to see how far they can carry their condemnation of slavery, without actually cutting themselves off
from religious association with the south.   The former class are
seeing how near they can come to the justification of slaveholding
without being actually identified with slaveholders: the latter,
how near they can come to its condemnation without being actually identified with abolitionists.

---

* I find this not in the Emancipator itself, but in another paper which
was put into my hands for another purpose.

"These latter gentlemen profess to hold the same views of slavery that they have always held. And perhaps, in many cases, they may be able to show where, ten or fifteen years ago, they expressed the same condemnation of slavery that they do now. The difference is, that formerly they came reluctantly to the expression of these views, lest they should be taken for abolitionists—now they do it eagerly, lest they should be deemed apologists for slavery. Formerly, they put forth their anti-slavery sentiments as an apology for acting against abolition; now they put forth their excuses for slaveholding as an apology for speaking against slavery.

"Of this class of theologians, no one has from the beginning come nearer to abolition without hitting it, than the Rev. Leonard Bacon, D. D., of New-Haven."

To such libels scattered broadcast over all the north, and proceeding from men who know me well, and who are known to have been once my friends, I expose myself when I utter my convictions on this subject. It seems not to enter into the thoughts of those writers, that a man who differs from them on this most complicated theme, may possibly be honest. My answer to their imputations is, Perhaps my motives are important to the question of the soundness of my arguments; perhaps you know my motives better than I do; yet God knows them better than you do; to my own master I stand or fall, and "with me it is a very small matter that I should be judged of you, or of man's judgment."

NO. VIII.

EXPLANATIONS.

I thought I had finished, when I appended to my last communication a postscript of condensed replies to those of my correspondents, known and unknown, whose inquiries or suggestions might seem to them not to have been sufficiently noticed heretofore. But as that postscript was not published in the last number of the Evangelist, and as the editors have thus left me at liberty to continue the discussion for another week, it seems proper to draw out the postscript into a concluding chapter of explanations. And this is the more important as the publication of my last week's essay brought me an immediate return of questions, some of which seem to show that my views are not yet, in all quarters, perfectly understood.

I. A correspondent in Ohio, who writes as a friend, though his name is to me that of a stranger, asks me to re-examine one position. The passage to which he refers is that in my second communication, which represents the burthen of proof as devolving upon those who shall hereafter bring certain accusations against our missionaries and churches among the Cherokees and Choctaws. This, he thinks, is a mistake. He says, " The fact of a man holding his fellow-man as property, *on the face of it appears wrong*. Let the Board, by proper explanations, show that these are cases of a peculiar character that exonerate those who do it from the charge of guilt. The missionaries are not a set of felors that we are trying to convict. *They are honest men, and we will give entire credit to their statements.* We only *ask for facts,* and will judge for ourselves. If we think they and the Board mistake in regard to their duty, we will say it in all kindness *as friends.* We shall not abandon the Board or the missionaries till we find they adopt as a *settled policy* the practice of admitting slaveholders to communion and church fellowship."

I have accordingly " re-examined" my position, and I find that my correspondent has quite mistaken my meaning. If he in his turn will " re-examine," he will see that what I say in that place is founded entirely on the explanations which the missionaries, and the Board as speaking in their behalf, *have given.* My position is this : Either the report made at Brooklyn, and since published, is entirely unworthy of credit as a representation of facts, or if there is in any church under the care of our missionaries a master who buys or sells human beings as merchandise—who does not recognize, in respect to his servants, the divine sanctity of their relations as husbands and wives, and as parents and children—who permits his servants to live and die in ignorance of God and of God's Word—who does not render to his servants that which is just and equal—or who refuses to acknowledge their dignity and worth as reasonable and immortal beings for whom Christ died—that master, upon being convicted of any such specification, " would be admonished by the church, and unless he should repent would be excommunicated." We have the declaration of the Board to this effect, founded upon the information received

11*

from their missionaries, and using to a considerable extent the very language of the missionaries themselves. From this time forward those who shall assume the responsibility of affirming the contrary, are bound to prove what they affirm.

But my friend says, " Give *us* the facts, in each case of slaveholding, and *we* will judge for ourselves." To me it seems that if we know the *principles* on which those missionaries and churches administer discipline, and if we have their comprehensive denial of all facts inconsistent with those principles, that is enough. Whether the facts in a particular case are such as show that a man is, in the judgment of charity, a Christian, acting in a Christian spirit, is a question upon which none are so well qualified to judge as that man's Christian neighbors, the very church with which he is in covenant. If my correspondent is charged with being a forger, on the ground that inasmuch as he is a skillful penman he has it in his power to commit forgery upon a sufficient temptation, and if I am therefore required to deny him fellowship, his denial of the charge is enough to put all who repeat it upon the duty of proving it. If the church to which he belongs is charged with admitting forgers to communion because it admits a man who can forge if he chooses, it is enough for that church to deny the charge and to demand the proof. Just so if a church is charged with admitting oppressors to communion because it admits " believing masters," who could oppress if they would, and who would be oppressors if the*j* were not believers, it is enough for that church to meet the charge with a denial. Such is the position of the Cherokee and

Choctaw churches and of the missionaries there; and such is the position of the Board.

It is to be observed here that the charge of admitting *slaveholders* to communion is not denied; but the charge of admitting *oppressors* to communion *is* denied comprehensively and in various specifications. So, in the case supposed, the church to which my correspondent belongs does not deny the charge of admitting to communion a man who can commit forgery if he will; it only denies the charge of admitting one who does commit forgery. If I can find reason to believe that a church in a slaveholding country will rigidly administer discipline against all specifications of oppression, I shall not doubt that the influence of that church will be as efficient for the promotion of freedom and of righteousness as if it were to excommunicate men simply for being slaveholders. As for the "settled policy" of the Board, I can only speak from my knowledge of the men and of the churches; but I think I may say that two points are immovably *settled;*—first, that the missionaries are never to permit any sort of oppression, on the part of those under their care as converts, to pass uncensured; and secondly, that no considerations of expediency, either political or ecclesiastical, will be deemed a sufficient reason for adopting a formula which would exclude from the missionary work the author of the first epistle to Timothy, and of the epistles to the Ephesians and Colossians.

II. The friend who writes to me from Maine, and whose ingenuousness I cannot question, has misconceived (and therefore I presume that others equally

candid have also misconceived) the meaning of the
note in which I answered a case of conscience about
a slave who runs away from the mere relation of
subjection to a master's confessedly beneficent authority.   In my understanding of the case, the master who conducts himself in that relation according
to the impulses of a Christian spirit, would readily
permit his slave to emigrate, if so disposed, and
would put him in the way of helping himself, so
that the necessity of the slave's *running* away to
avoid what might happen in case of his master's
death, and the consequent necessity of his throwing
himself on the sympathies of abolitionists as a men-
dicant, would not exist.

III. Another, writing from a village in Central
New York, wishes me to "discuss two questions."
"Does the law of love plainly *require* any master to
control the services of his servant, against his will,
without reward, during his (the servant's) life? If
not, does the law of love plainly *permit* the master
to control the services of his servant, against his
will, without reward, during his life?"

To *discuss* these questions in detail might exhaust
the patience of those who are waiting to reply to
me.   I can only give my opinion.   (1.) The law of
love requires every master to render to his slaves,
in the best practicable form, a just equivalent for all
their service.   He may not be able to render that
equivalent in the form of wages, and he may err in
judging what wages he would have to pay them in
a state of freedom; for the theory of fair wages supposes that the laborer and employer are at once
mutually dependent and mutually independent;

and the rate of wages, *i. e.*, the price of labor, *i. e.*, the share which labor is to have in the division of what is the joint product of labor, skill and capital, is determined, just as the price of any other commodity is determined, by the state of the market. But no conscientious man will consider himself entitled to use the services of his fellow-men, simply because he has power over them, without rendering to them what he in his conscience regards as a just equivalent. Such equivalent *may* be rendered in the form of food, clothing, house-rent, protection, and an accumulating fund as in a savings bank, which is ultimately to establish the slaves as free in some free country. Or it *may* be rendered in some other way. (2.) I hold that the law of love requires the master to regard the relation between himself and his slaves as a relation to be dissolved as soon as it can be done consistently with the welfare of the slaves. If one slave and another dies before that time arrives, it is analogous to the case of an apprentice dying in his minority. The master's right to maintain the relation, for the protection and government of the slave, as long as the slave lives, unless the slave chooses to become free by emigration, is far less doubtful than his right to maintain it till his own death shall throw them into the hands of his heirs or of his creditors.

IV. In my description of a case of actual slave-holding, there was a sentence which has excited a violent curiosity in the mind of the "fellow sinner," who, under various signatures, has favored me with several communications, the first of which was the

case of conscience. Of the master whom I described,
I said, "The discipline on his plantation is not
lax, but strict; his people are in every respect orderly, and are obliged to be so." These few words
raise in my correspondent's mind "visions of over-
seers and cowskins;" and he desires me to tell him
whether I "witnessed a Christian flagellation laid
on according to apostolical sanction." Frankly, then,
I witnessed no such thing. And furthermore, in all
that I have said about applying "discipline," "strict
discipline," in the church, to those who are guilty of
certain offences, I do not mean such discipline as
has been used against heretics in Spain, nor do I demand that the offenders shall be flogged with "cowskins."   And if, in describing the management of a
Christian shipmaster, setting it in contrast with that
of many a rough and brutal captain, I should say,
"The discipline on board his vessel is not lax, but
strict; his men are in every respect orderly, and are
obliged to be so," I should not mean that he has no
method of maintaining order and discipline, but by
the rope's end.   Or if, in describing a schoolmaster
as very unlike those of the tribe of Mr. Squeers, I
should say, "The discipline in his school is not lax,
but strict; the boys are in every respect orderly, and
are obliged to be so," I should not mean that he is
in the habit of whipping and kicking his pupils.
Discipline is not of course cruelty.

V. From another correspondent I have received
several inquiries—of which he says, "These are
practical questions, and I presume there are many
who would like to know how you would answer

them." I will, therefore, answer his questions as briefly as I can, in the order in which he proposes them.

1. He asks whether, if a clergyman from the south should come to New Haven, and should be commonly reported to be a slaveholder, I would regard that reputation as *prima facie* evidence against him, and would, on that account, refuse to invite him to my pulpit. To this I answer, that as matters now stand, in respect to discipline in the southern churches, I should delay asking a slaveholder, or one commonly reputed to be such, to preach for me, till, either by friendly conference, or in some other way, I had obtained such knowledge of him as would enable me to believe that he is endeavoring honestly, and in the fear of God, to render to his servants that which is just and equal. But after obtaining satisfaction on this point, I should have no scruple whatever. The difficulty is, that as matters now are, the fact of a man's being a Presbyterian minister at the south in ever so high standing, is not of itself sufficient evidence, nor is it even *prima facie* evidence, of his being free from very gross sins; such as making merchandise of men, women and children, who happen to be placed helpless in his power; or sundering the husband and wife, the parents and their child; or compelling them to toil for him all their lives long, without once asking himself conscientiously what he owes them for their toil; or leaving them to the tender mercies of a wicked overseer, who cares not for their welfare or their rights. Therefore, as in the case of a minister from Germany, the official certificates of his ordination and of his unim-

peached standing would be no evidence of his not
being a rationalist; and as in the case of a minister
from the Church of England, the official certificates
of his ordination and of his unimpeached standing
would be no proof of his making any profession of
what we call evangelical piety; so in the case of a
minister from certain regions of the south, the like
certificates would be no conclusive evidence of his
not being an oppressor of his fellow-men. I do, indeed, know a slaveholder who often preaches for me,
and whose slaveholding is not the least scandal in
my eyes. If the south were well supplied with just
such ministers as he is, we might hope to see great
changes there.

2. My friend also inquires whether, if a layman,
reputed to be a slaveholder, should offer himself for
admission to my church, I would admit him without
an examination on the point of his slaveholding. I
answer, that in respect to *occasional* communion, we
are not accustomed to make any examination of
strangers professing to be Christians, who happen to
be present in our assemblies. But admission to
membership is another affair; and if one reputed to
be a master of slaves should offer himself, we should
desire to know how he performs his duties toward
those ignorant, unprotected, helpless men, so absolutely committed to his power. We should certainly
desire to know whether he is treating them according to the law of love, or whether he is treating
them as property.

3. Another question is, whether I would employ
slaveholders as missionaries, either at home or in
foreign countries. I think that when God qualifies

and calls a southern slaveholder to preach the
gospel, he does not often call such a man to Africa
or China. Let him preach at home, and if he will
preach faithfully, and administer discipline faithfully, so far as the administration of discipline is in
his hands, I see no reason why we should not help
him if he needs assistance. It is by the labor of
just such men on their native southern soil that
slavery is to be abolished.

There is one more point of explanation to which,
in conclusion, I would ask the attention of the
reader. Some may think that in my theory of how
Christianity may and will operate for the extinction
of slavery, a great amount of time is required,
whereas we want, and ought to have, some quicker
process. Undoubtedly slavery ought to be abolished
much sooner than it is likely to be; but how can we
abolish it? The problem of the abolition of slavery
in this country is altogether unlike the now accomplished problem of the abolition of slavery in the
British colonies. The abolition of slavery was
imposed upon Jamaica and Demarara, and the other
British countries at this side of the Atlantic, by an
extrinsic physical force which could not be resisted.
How long would the abolition of slavery in those
countries have been deferred if it had waited for the
spontaneous action of the colonial legislative assemblies? Had Jamaica been an independent state
—had its laws been simply the expression of the
judgments and sentiments entertained by its white
population, what could have been effected there by
political and religious agitation in Great Britain
—liberty tickets—Exeter Hall speeches—votes of

the Congregational Union or of the London Missionary Society? The slaveholding States in the American confederation, considered as States, are free ; no Imperial Parliament can dictate laws to them. The abolition of slavery can be imposed upon them from without by no other agency than war—an agency which I do not believe the anti-slavery societies or their members expect to employ. In those States, then, the abolition of slavery, if effected by any peaceful process, will take place only as the result of a change in the people there —a change which shall make them recognize the slave as a man—a change which shall make them understand and feel that a free black peasant, laboring for wages and taking care of himself, is a practicable thing, and is every way a better thing, more sightly to the eye, more agreeable to the moral sense, more safe and profitable to the landholder and to the State, than a slave laboring under the lash of a driver, and taken care of as a horse is by his owner. The true problem for anti-slavery philanthrophy is, how to effect that change in the minds and hearts of the southern people—that change in their judgments and affections—out of which the legislative abolition must proceed. And to me it seems that either that moral and intellectual change must be despaired of entirely, or the chief agent in effecting it must be Christianity, under such an administration of it as, in these communications, I have attempted to describe ;—not Christianity in the form of law concerning itself with outward civil relations, but the Christianity of light and love—the Christianity of spiritual indi-

vidual regeneration, recognizing as Christians all
those, and only those, who give evidence of loving
God, and of loving their neighbors as themselves.